POLISHING

FRENCH POLISHING

PHILIPPA BARSTOW
ALAN WATERHOUSE

B.T. BATSFORD LTD · LONDON

VIDEO

Published together with this book is a video, made by Find A Fact Limited, in which Alan Waterhouse and Philippa Barstow demonstrate how to put into practice many of the techniques described in the book. For details of availability, please see page 151.

First published 1993, reprinted 1995
Published in paperback 1997

Typeset by J&L Composition Ltd,
Filey, North Yorkshire

and printed in Hong Kong

Published by
B.T. Batsford Ltd
583 Fulham Road
London SW6 5BY

A catalogue record for this book is available from the British Library

ISBN 0 7134 8261 3

ACKNOWLEDGEMENTS

Robert Barstow for his diligence in proof reading the manuscripts.

To all the people who taught us the love of furniture and the skills we use today.

To all past, present and future students who help to make work a pleasant, interesting but fraught life.

Black and white photographs and cover by Prakash Measuria of Ashton-under-Lyne, Lancashire.

Figures 13, 53, 60, 62, 67–84, 96 and 146 by Graham Holland of Eccles, Lancashire.

Figures 1–3, 11, 40–1 and 49 by Sid Richards of Design House of Marple Bridge, Cheshire.

Contents

Part Three: Projects 113

I NTRODUCTION

We have written this book for the many people who want to learn the art of French polishing, and also for those with some experience already, who want to learn more about the tips and techniques of the professional French polisher. So many people are put off because the process seems mystifying and therefore daunting: we aim to dispel that apprehension and bring French polishing within reach of all those with an interest in furniture, and hope there will be something here for everyone.

First and foremost, we have tried to answer the problems and doubts commonly raised by our students setting out to polish or repolish a piece of furniture, whether old or new. The advantage of French polishing is that it is a very practical sequence of work and follows very logical steps which allow even an absolute novice to obtain a very pleasing finish, and to improve on that increasingly with more experience.

By explaining the history of different types of finishes and suitable methods of work for each (whether cleaning or repolishing) this book will help you to assess the requirements of each individual piece of furniture, and to work logically to a high standard. To this end we have included photographs, drawings and tables.

Students of polishing will need patience, perseverance and the ability to stop if a problem arises, think about it (and refer to the appropriate chapter if necessary), then pick up the work and carry on again. Remember: furniture restoration is a skill that needs practice, a craft that needs understanding and an art that needs an appreciation of beauty.

We refer throughout the book to the techniques and materials that we ourselves use regularly. All the materials are readily obtainable, and they do work. See the list of suppliers at the back for further details.

PART ONE
PREPARATION

1

A BRIEF HISTORY OF FURNITURE AND FINISHES

The history of furniture is divided into various periods; usually by monarchs, the designers and makers, or the popular timbers in use during that time.

From a wood finisher's point of view there are clearly defined periods in which certain materials were used. As a general guide:

Between 1500 and 1700 furniture was given a protective application of oil (nut, poppy or linseed being the most common), beeswax or paint, and over many years of care and attention a patina was obtained to bring a very pleasing, hardwearing surface much sought-after by collectors.

Between 1700 and 1820 copal varnish was widely used and was generally waxed afterwards, though wax or oiling alone remained in general use. From about the middle of the eighteenth century French polish was also used, among the first to employ this being the French Ebonists. Its use then spread throughout Europe and North America in the later part of the nineteenth century.

By 1820 French polishing had become a recognized trade in Britain as increasing industrialization called for faster methods of finishing, which French polishing offered.

By the 1840s and 1850s French polishing had become the standard method of finishing furniture; this carried on until the 1930s.

In the 1930s modern finishing methods such as spraying cellulose became the norm until the present day when only a small percentage of furniture is polished by hand.

The age of oak

This covers the period from the fifteenth century to the late seventeenth century when the majority of furniture was made by joiners who were also house builders and used oak and other local timbers. There were two reasons for this: first, oak was the main timber available in large quantities and in large enough sections to use for house building; and second, there were very few specialist furniture makers so it fell to the local joiner to make furniture for the houses he built, and he would naturally use the timbers he was familiar with.

The earliest known method of finishing consisted of oiling the wood with poppy or nut oil, which was sometimes dyed by the immersion of alkanet root in the oil for a few days before use. The oil was applied so that it thoroughly penetrated the grain of the wood and was then left to harden by exposure to air. Beeswax was then dissolved in pure turpentine to form a thick paste which was then rubbed into the pores and polished by repeated friction with a brush. After each operation, lasting some hours, the piece was allowed to stand for a day to allow the turpentine to evaporate and the wax to harden.

This process could be repeated at intervals over a long period of time and there is no doubt that Tudor and early Stuart oak furniture was periodically 'renovated' in this way. This lengthy process has produced timber of beautiful colour resembling fine old bronze with a glossy surface.

It is interesting to note from a polisher's point of view that when removing this patina, it is actually a very thin film of dirt and polish.

The age of walnut

This period spans roughly 1680–1740. With increasing skills among furniture makers, particularly in Europe, walnut became the common timber for good furniture. When William and Mary ascended the English throne in 1688, they brought with them continental craftsmen and fashions. Walnut, which is a finer-grained timber than oak, was then crafted in subtle shapes and patterns previously unseen in oak pieces. The extensive use of veneers and inlays, and increased affluence and elegance, also strongly influenced furniture of the time.

During this age of walnut demand from the commercial classes meant that the older methods of oiling or waxing furniture were found to be too time-consuming and expensive. The method then adopted was to varnish the wood with copal varnish applied with a brush. Copal varnish appears to have been made from gum copal (from the *rhus copallinum* or *sumach* of Spanish America) dissolved in boiling oil (most probably poppy oil).

Due to pressure to produce furniture quickly, oiling before varnishing was omitted as the oil needed too much time to dry properly before applying the varnish (or the varnish would split and crack).

Instead, two or three coats of thin varnish would be applied, each being allowed to dry thoroughly before the next was brushed on. To finish with it would be waxed as before.

This new method had its critics, and according to Cescinsky in *English Furniture in the Eighteenth Century* (1909):

> This previous varnishing of the wood had the effect of considerably shortening the process of polishing, but it was open to several grave objections. Writers on this subject have frequently commented on the liability of walnut to the attacks of worms, a liability equally shared by birch, sycamore, beech, chestnut, pear or lime, but no one appears to have noticed that these woods in their natural state are seldom affected in this way. The supposition that the worms are attracted by the resinous varnish is, therefore, exceedingly strong, especially when it is remembered that Tudor oak is comparatively free from this kind of ravage, unless it has been varnished.

Fine Queen Anne walnut in its original state has a rich amber colour, due to the covering varnish and this is lost if the piece is scraped and repolished.

The age of mahogany (The age of the designer)

By 1730 walnut had become scarce because of severe frosts in Europe, while mahogany had begun to arrive in England from the West Indies, initially as ballast for ships involved in the three world trade of Europe, Africa and the West Indies. The mahogany came mainly from Cuba and San Domingo, hence the description Spanish mahogany as these were Spanish Colonies. Exotic timbers such as satinwood, ebony and rosewood were introduced later on in the period in decorative work.

This period from 1730 until about 1820 is also referred to as the age of the designer due to the changing nature of the furniture world. Increasingly plentiful, mahogany was regarded as a rich timber that could be crafted into beautiful furniture due to its working properties and the growth of the craftsman sector (many coming into England from Europe). There was greater opulence in England and many craftsmen had rich patrons who commissioned many items of furniture. House design was also changing and many more rooms were used than during the age of oak, so both the

Fig 1 A Chippendale design carver dining chair. Note the C scrolls on the inside of the leg's knee and the pierced splat back which are common to Chippendale designs. Many less elegant copies have been made but conform to the basic elements of design

Fig 2 A Hepplewhite camel back dining chair. After the shield back design the camel back is probably the best known Hepplewhite design. The style is more restrained than Chippendale and incorporates more straight lines

alike all over England and beyond were able to copy his designs (Fig. 1).

George Hepplewhite (died 1786) A designer and cabinet maker who worked in London. His style was elegant and refined and is particularly noted for chairs (Fig. 2) and settees with shield backs, some incorporating the Prince of Wales's feathers. He also published a book of his designs called *The Cabinet Maker and Upholsterer's Guide.*

Thomas Sheraton (1751–1806) Designer of delicate furniture, often with marquetry. He began as a working cabinet maker but made very little furniture. He published books of furniture towards the end of the eighteenth and the first years of the nineteenth centuries, his most important being *The Cabinet Maker, Upholsterer and General Artist's Encyclopedia.* His designs were widely copied (Fig. 3).

Robert Adam (1728–1792) Adam came from a family of architects, his father William an Edinburgh architect. Along with his brothers James, John and William he set up a London practice. Some of his more famous buildings include 20 Portman Square, London and Kedleston Hall near Derby. He believed that the whole of a building and its contents should conform to a unified design – thus he concerned himself with the interior decoration and accessories such as furniture, fireplaces and door fittings. His influence can still be seen today with the current vogue for 'Adam style' fireplaces.

London became the centre for designers and architects and as a result of the circulation of books by people such as Chippendale the designs became available to a large number of people across Europe

volume and range of furniture increased. Designers became increasingly popular as they designed both houses and the furniture to go into them. Many designers were not actually skilled craftsmen but they employed a large number of skilled people. Such designers included:

Thomas Chippendale (1718–1789) Very possibly the most famous name in English furniture. He spent most of his life in London and published many of his furniture designs in a book called *The Gentleman and Cabinet Maker's Guide* from which cabinet makers and joiners

and ultimately North America. Often items copied from the books would be inferior in quality but many examples still survive today.

Copal varnish was superseded by a polish composed of gum—lac, *coccus lacca*, dissolved in spirit of wine. This was faster drying and was still applied with a brush. The modern method of applying with a rubber and using oil for lubrication was unknown. The pores would not have been filled with polishing but subsequent years of waxing and handling would have filled the grain.

According to Cescinsky in *English Furniture in the Eighteenth Century*:

> This early polish is exceedingly hard, partly due to the action of time, but chiefly owing to its application without previous oiling of the wood and in very thin coats. It is comparatively easy to detect original polishes especially if the surface is scraped; modern French polish flakes off, the original powders away, the particles being light in colour like powered resin and possess a similar aroma.

In North America at this time the European influence can be seen where native American timbers such as maple were used with a mixture of European design details.

The Georgian era

In this era, covering the reigns of the four Georges (1714–1830), furniture followed architectural lines and mahogany became the most widely used timber. Brass and ebony were increasingly used for decoration, as were motifs such as sabre legs and rope backs commemorating Lord Nelson and the Anglo-French naval battles of the Napoleonic era. By 1820 shellac (French polish) was also in use with very thin applications to seal the wood and protect

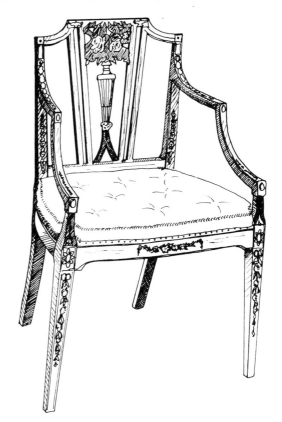

Fig 3 A Sheraton style chair of great elegance and delicacy. Sheraton is renowned for inlaid furniture, though in some cases the 'inlay' may have been painted on to simulate the real thing

Fig 4 A Georgian mahogany tray that had been polished originally with a thin polish and then waxed

it before waxing (Fig. 4). Unfortunately, almost nothing is known about the individuals or companies involved in the nascent French polishing industry.

At about the same time as the introduction of French polishing, the method of staining mahogany with bichromate of potash dissolved in water came into practice. This stain both darkens and reddens mahogany, in contrast to unstained, varnished, eighteenth century mahogany which varies from a golden to a brown shade but is never red.

Strong sunlight over a great many years will have faded unstained mahogany but the fading will be even and generally produces a golden shade which is brilliant and clear. Mahogany which was originally stained with bichromate of potash will be bleached by years of exposure to the sun but will be patchy and opaque.

The Victorian era

With the accession of the young Victoria to the throne in 1837 the trend in furniture became feminine and delicate. The timber used during the early years of her reign was walnut, with a strong French influence on style. It was generally polished a natural colour to suit the delicate nature of the designs.

At about the same time manufacturing on a large scale became general, woodworking machinery having already been used for about 30 years. This machinery and other innovations of the industrial revolution meant that the making of furniture became a manufacturing process rather than the work of an individual craftsman. Much of the work was still done by hand but increasingly by semi-skilled people or non-craftsmen doing only one part of the process.

Manufacturers became less selective in their choice of timber in order to keep costs down. Inferior timbers were often used for the sides of furniture and then the polisher had to colour match these pieces to imitate better timber of a predetermined shade. Water based stains and earth colours were introduced to enable a wider range of finished colours to be achieved. The natural colour was therefore no longer the only colour. Oak was the timber most often used and would frequently be fumed in stables and then thinly polished so that the grain and quality of the wood showed.

William Morris and the Arts and Crafts Movement tried to stem what they saw as the onslaught of the industrial revolution by promoting individual skills and better selection of timbers, but the mass market continued to grow along with the population in the industrial towns and cities across Britain (Figs. 5–6).

In the late 1880s reproduction furniture became quite widespread as high quality Chippendale and Tudor furniture was extensively copied, and they are now desirable pieces in their own right. The Tudor style furniture was generally stained very dark with water stain and then French polished to simulate age. Just before Queen Victoria's death in 1901 the most popular trend of reproduction furniture was the Sheraton style, while Art Nouveau led the way among modern styles. As with all styles and fashions, they began by being of high quality but fell victim to cheaper and less well-made imitations as time passed.

Twentieth century

In the 1920s Chippendale and Hepplewhite mahogany were popular reproduction styles while oak was used in modern designs. By the 1930s oak was still popular but mahogany had been replaced by walnut, often enhanced with attractive veneers. By the end of the decade cellulose sprayed finishes had become the norm on mass-produced furniture.

The arrival of war in 1939 meant that Utility furniture became almost the only furniture available, using practical designs which were easy to manufacture and economic on materials but nonetheless of a very good standard. The predominant timbers were oak, beech and mahogany. Fifty years later some pieces of Utility furniture are still regarded as well-made, well-designed and useful pieces of furniture. Quite recently we have had a number of pieces through our workshop for restoration.

With the end of Utility furniture in the 1950s came the fashion for veneered walnut furniture, with curved or bowed doors as the main feature and polished to a high gloss with cellulose lacquer. The 1960s saw the arrival of the Scandinavian influence of teak furniture with its very plain, practical, clean lines.

The introduction of chipboard and very thin veneers meant that design was increasingly based on plain flat boards. Design has become governed by the capabilities of mass production i.e. the design has been made to suit the product rather than suiting the timber to the design.

Current mass produced furniture is generally knock-down so that it can be made from boards cut to a standard size and the finish applied by roller coating or curtain coating before being packed into boxes for self-assembly.

Fig 5   A late Victorian inlaid walnut music Canterbury. The original finish was polish and varnish (a cheap but fast way of polishing a job)

Fig 6   A walnut nineteenth century chair, more recently painted white. It would have been French polished originally

2

SHELLAC AND
FRENCH POLISHES

Origins of lac

Lac, the resin, is excreted by the insect *Laciffer Lacoa*, from which shellac is produced. The insect is a parasite living in certain trees in India and other Eastern countries, and India is the biggest exporter of the world's lac requirements. The insect is orange-red and about 1.25mm (1/20in) long, and has a life cycle of about six months. It covers the twigs and leaves of certain trees with a protective coat of resin. The male dies after the fertilization of the female, and upon death both male and female insects are trapped in the resin. The lac, when gathered (stick lac), contains the dead insects and impurities from the bark of the tree.

Manufacture of shellac

The lac is gathered by cutting the infected twigs from the trees and then scraping the lac off the twigs. Once the lac has been removed from the twigs it is washed with water to remove the particles of twigs and other impurities; and on drying it is know as seed lac. This is put into canvas tubes and heated over a fire. One end of the tube is fixed and the other rotated to squeeze the molten shellac through the hessian as it melts. The initial shellac that comes through is clean and small amounts are dropped onto cold stone, where it sets in the form of a thin disc up to about 75mm (3in) in diameter. This is known as button lac from which button polish is made. The next amount of shellac that oozes through may contain impurities which would easily be detected visually if the shellac was in the form of a button and it is, therefore, stretched into a thin sheet and crushed, when cold, into flakes. It is from these flakes that which French polish is made.

White and transparent shellac is made by dissolving the seed lac in a hot caustic solution of water and then bleaching the solution with chlorine. After bleaching the caustic is neutralized with an acid, which causes the shellac to precipitate out of solution. In this form it is known as bleached shellac. Bleaching shellac alters its chemical properties so that unless it is dissolved in alcohol within three or four days after bleaching it will become insoluble.

Shellac contains a very small amount of wax from the insect. The wax is insoluble in alcohol and causes the cloudiness which can often be seen settling towards the bottom of the container. Transparent shellac is made by removing the wax from the bleached shellac and washing it with petroleum solvent which dissolves the wax but not the shellac.

French polish This is both a proper and collective noun. As a collective noun it covers all polishes made with shellac and alcohol. As a proper noun it refers to one specific type of material made from flake shellac and alcohol. It consists of approximately 1–1.5kg (2.5–3lb) of shellac to 5l (1gal) of alcohol. The alcohol used can be 64 or 66 overproof industrial alcohol.

The type of shellac used can also vary considerably, both in its quality and its colour.

Button polish This is made from button shellac, that is shellac in the shape of buttons of approximately 75mm (3in) diameter. This shellac is harder and more orange in colour than flake shellac which is used to manufacture French polish. The method of application is the same as with French polish. The button polish we use is 4lb button meaning that 1.8kg (4lb) of button shellac is dissolved in 5l (1 gal) of alcohol. Button polish is superior to French polish but it can impart a slight colour to the wood.

White polish This is a French polish made from bleached white shellac. The action of bleaching shellac alters its properties slightly and white French polish does not dry as quickly as ordinary French polish. If kept in stock too long its drying time becomes even more prolonged. We would never recommend the use of this polish as it is too soft and does not wear well. Traditionally this polish would be used where a transparent finish was required but this polish has been superseded by the more recent introduction of heat resisting pale polish, as detailed below.

Heat resisting pale polish This is a relatively recent introduction and it is an almost transparent French polish, the shellac having been modified with urea or thio urea to make it more resistant to heat than any of the other polishes above. We recommend and use it particularly for table tops or any other surface which gets quite a lot of wear. We also use it where we want to keep the timber as natural a colour as possible.

Garnet polish Made to a dark red (garnet) colour, this polish was used mostly in the earlier parts of the twentieth century to give a warmer, darker colour to mahogany and oak furniture. At that time oak was generally either polished with a high shine to a dark shade, or lightly stained and not highly polished with transparent polish. The reason that garnet polish was used is that after staining button polish gave a yellowy/brown cast to the surface, making it look cloudy. Whereas the garnet polish, being darker, actually gave the grain greater clarity.

Nowadays, if we wanted the same result, we would tint button polish with spirit red and black, but we only tend to use such a tinted polish at the colouring stage. We do find, however, that by mixing our oil-based stains to the required colour and using clear polishes we get a better result than we would from garnet polish, as the whole object of French polishing these days is to produce a finish with as great a clarity of the grain as possible, unlike most mass produced furniture, which is finished with a tinted lacquer that tends to obscure the grain.

3

WORKSHOP AND CONDITIONS

Creating the best environment

In order to achieve the best results you need a good working environment which should include:

- as much natural light as possible
- a good heating system
- plenty of ventilation
- a clean workshop

If you work in a dirty and cramped workshop you will find it inconvenient and it will ultimately take you longer to polish a job. You will also not achieve the best results that are within your capabilities. Take your time and get your workshop organized before commencing polishing.

Make things as easy as possible for yourself – we do all our polishing now on a carpeted floor and have a thorough clean out every week. Ensure that all materials and tools are conveniently placed. Place your work bench in a convenient spot, close to natural light.

We will tend to spend one day stripping and papering furniture so that all the dirty jobs are done at the same time. This means that the following day the workshop can be cleaned and polishing can commence. We never work so that one is papering when the other is finishing off. If you share the workshop with someone else, try to coordinate your activities to keep dust to a minimum while you are polishing.

Plenty of natural light Side light is preferable to overhead light. If artificial light is the only source of light you have available we would suggest normal electric filament bulbs rather than fluorescent, as the latter has two distinct disadvantages:

- it gives a greenish tint i.e. red looks browner beneath it
- if the direction of the wood grain is the same as the length of the light it is more difficult to see the surface clearly, particularly when removing raw linseed oil at the finishing stage

Fig 7   Collapsible trestles: because of the top rail they will not 'walk'

A good heating system A working temperature of around 65°F (18°C) will normally be sufficient. If your workshop is too warm the polish may dry too quickly so that polishing large areas will become more difficult. If it is cold and damp you will have problems with the polish chilling, i.e. a milky film will appear.

Clean conditions and a good ventilation system A wall-mounted extractor fan helps to remove dust as well as fumes. Fumes should not cause a problem if you ensure that your workshop is well-ventilated. But dust can have a harmful effect on the lungs, so use a dust mask. The dust arising from sanding is very carcinogenic so even the most basic dust mask will save you from problems in later life.

Fig 8   Bench pads protect polished work

A metal storage cupboard For flammable materials.

A suitable workbench We use sets of folding trestles and loose boards. If you

have trestles of different heights you should find the ideal height for all jobs. A selection of different size boards also helps. Choose a board that can be turned over so one side can be used for dirty

Fig 9 Some of our cramps and glues

work e.g. stripping and staining, and the other side can be kept clean for polishing (Fig. 7).

Sets of bench pads of differing sizes These are essential when turning polished work over. These are pieces of wood of any suitable size covered with fabric (Fig. 8).

Clothing You will need:

- good quality rubber gloves
- a large woodworking apron that covers your clothes
- an old pair of shoes with thick soles
- old clothes, as you must expect to get dirty even when wearing an apron

A selection of woodworking and other tools   (Fig. 9)

For Stripping

- paint or cabinet scraper
- a wire brush
- tins to work from
- old paint brushes to apply stripper
- grade 3 steel wool
- rubber gloves

For Repairing and Preparation

- chisels of various sizes
- saws (tenon, fret etc.)
- cramps (G, sash and webbing)
- drill and bits
- pliers and pincers
- screwdrivers of assorted sizes
- screws and panel pins
- nail punch
- hammer and mallet
- various glues
- garnet paper and cork block
- epoxy filler or plastic stopper
- cabinet scrapers
- dust mask

For Removing Upholstery

- ripping chisel
- mallet
- staple remover
- pincers and pliers
- nail punch
- hammer
- dust mask

For Polishing

- pipe smoker's penknife
- Zorino mops and quills
- pot or glass containers to work from
- wadding and cotton cloth

Fig 10 The authors contemplating work – note how everything is easily to hand

Safety

The greatest potential danger to be faced in the workshop is fire, as all polishing materials are flammable. Suitable fire extinguishers are essential and should be clearly visible and within easy reach should the occasion arise.

Note: Be sure to have a choice of fire-extinguisher. While water-based extinguishers are good for general fires, they are not suitable for oil or electrical fires. Halon and CO_2 extinguishers are only really effective against electrical fires. Powder extinguishers are a must in the workshop as they are particularly effective against oil and petrol fires.

Certain materials should only be handled whilst wearing gloves: e.g. oxalic acid, stripper, oil stains and ammonia water, to name a few. With stripper we recommend wearing a long-sleeved shirt to avoid accidental splashing on the arm.

If you are susceptible to skin irritation a barrier cream is advisable. Methyl chloride stripper and turpentine-based liquids seem to cause the greatest problems, so wear good quality rubber gloves.

Storage and use of materials

The range of materials a polisher needs is relatively small and can be kept easily to hand (Fig. 10). It is essential that you store and use them correctly.

Highly flammable materials e.g. methyl chloride stripper, methylated spirit, oil stains and all polishes are best stored in a metal cupboard, away from a heat source.

Garnet papers need to be stored flat and in dry conditions. If they get damp during storage dry them out before use or they will not be effective.

Stripper is supplied in metal containers. When you wish to use stripper pour it into a suitable size tin can to work from – never use plastic as stripper will easily rot it, and do not use china or glass containers as they will be etched. See Chapter 6.

Polishes are supplied in stout plastic containers and when you are using them a small straight-sided cup or glass container is suitable. (You can also use this for mixing colour when required.)

Oil-based stains are supplied in metal containers, and when applying small quantities of stain, pour it into a tin can, never into a plastic container as the stain will rot it within minutes. Always use rubber gloves when handling stains: fine surgical gloves are no use as the stain will soon rot them, so choose washing-up gloves or even stouter ones for protection.

Note: The containers you work from should each be kept for one purpose: i.e. keep separate metal containers for stripper and oil stain, and reserve glass and china containers for polish or colour.

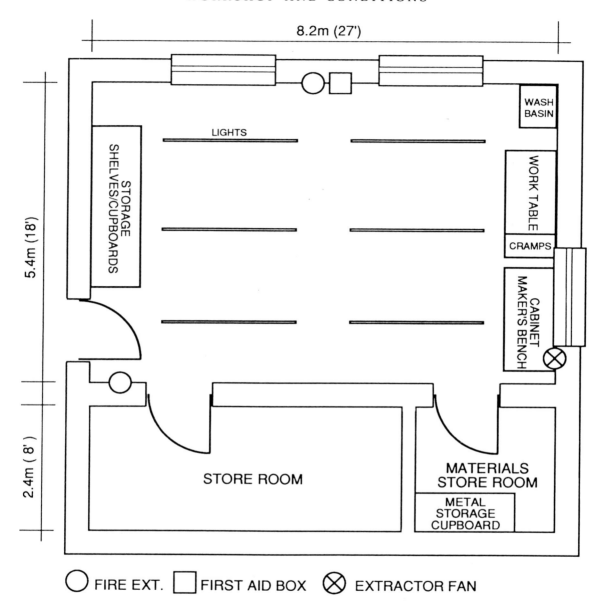

Fig 11 Plan for workshop. As much natural light as possible is desirable as natural light is preferable to artificial light. Situate cabinet bench near to a window and always ensure that fire extinguishers and first aid boxes are within easy reach

On the move

When we are working on site, be it in a public house or a court of law, we take a kit box containing all the materials we require. In fact, we have two kit boxes, one containing stripping, timber preparation and staining materials, and the other containing polishing materials.

Our boxes are wooden with a carrying handle. They have a front opening which will act as a tray to hold the materials and to minimize damage if they are spilled (Fig. 12).

Fig 12   Our portable work boxes, containing everything we might need when working on site

Cleaning hands after work

Although we always try to work as cleanly as possible when polishing, hands do get dirty. We clean them by putting a table-spoon of 0.880 ammonia into about 2.5l (½gal) of hot water and using a piece of towel; this removes all polishes and stains quite easily. Afterwards, wash your hands in clean water.

You can further utilize this ammonia water to clean all your pot and glass jars: put them in the water and leave them overnight. Rinse them in clean water in the morning and they will be ready to be used again. Note that normal household soda will be just as effective as the ammonia in the same circumstances.

4

*T*RADITIONAL
POLISHING
A QUICK REFERENCE

This is our recommended sequence of operations to follow when polishing or repolishing a piece of furniture in the traditional way (French polishing): some parts may be left out but the sequence should not be altered. It is intended only as a quick reference guide, and the following chapters provide more detailed explanation.

Cleaning – if stripping is not required

Dirt, grease, old wax etc. may be removed as follows:

A Raw linseed oil and pure turpentine (or turpentine substitute) in equal measures. (Apply with a soft cloth and use fine grade steel wool (0000 grade) to remove the dirt.)

B Oil, pure turpentine and methylated spirit in equal measures. Apply as **A**.

C Weak ammonia and hot water. Apply with towelling then clean off with clean water.

D Weak soda and hot water. Apply as **C**.

E Weak soda and hot water and scouring powder. Sprinkle the scouring powder on the damp towelling after dipping it in the weak soda solution.

Note: The first method **A** is the mildest and the last **E** the most severe, so if you are unsure of the degree of cleaning required start with the mildest.

PROGRESS NOW TO COLOURING

Stripping

This should be carried out in the following sequence:

1 Apply methyl chloride stripper as per manufacturer's instructions using an old paint brush of appropriate size.
2 Allow time for chemical reaction (approximately 10 minutes).
3a If old polish is soft, scrape clean with a paint scraper, putting waste into old newspaper.
3b If old polish is not soft, re-coat with stripper and repeat procedures **2** and **3**.
4 Re-apply stripper and remove all old polish and dirt with grade 3 steel wool.
5 Neutralize with warm ammonia water (only if solid wood), methylated spirit, turpentine substitute or cellulose thinners. Apply any of the neutralizing agents evenly with towelling, covering small areas as they will evaporate quickly.
6 Rub off with clean grade 3 steel wool or a fine wire brush for moulds or carvings.

Preparation

1 Carry out all repairs, fill holes and faults using epoxy resin or Brummer stopping as required.
2 Paper down (using a cork block on flat areas) with 80, 100, 120 or 150 grade garnet paper. Start with the coarser paper (i.e. 80 grade) and work through to the finer papers. For veneers finish with a fine grade (e.g. 150 grade grit).
3 Apply stain with towelling or wadding. Make sure you have selected the right type of stain for the job and check the drying time for each type of stain used.
4 Wipe off evenly in the direction of the grain using clean towelling.
5 If you have used water stain allow to dry for 24 hours then lightly paper down with a fine paper until it is smooth (as the water will have raised the grain). Take care when papering not to sand through the colour.

Note: Never use more than one type of stain on any job.

6 If grain filler is to be applied choose the appropriate colour and use hessian or curtaining to rub off the surplus and leave to dry.
7 'Seal' the stain and/or filler with a coat of shellac sealer using a good quality brush (mop). Alternatively 'seal' with polish using a fad (i.e. a rubber without a rag over it) when a thin polish is required or where the area is too large to coat with a brush.

Colouring

The surface now requires a smooth, clean working area ready for colouring: this is obtained as follows:

1 Fill any small holes or imperfections with coloured beeswax.
2 Paper down smooth with 150 grade or an old piece of 120 grade garnet paper. Alternatively use a sanding pad.
3 To provide the required surface give a rubber of polish approximately 4 times

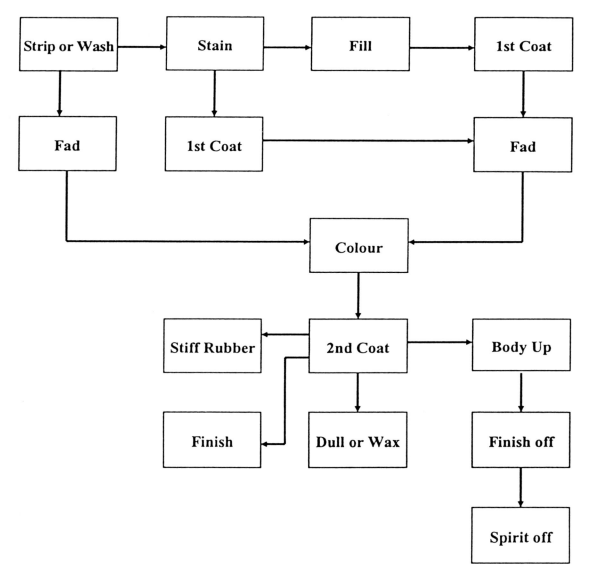

Fig 13 The chart shows the sequences to take. You can miss out sequences but you must not alter them

over the work. Then assess the areas to be coloured. Start with the minor areas, mixing sufficient colour, using polish and methylated spirit in equal measures as a base.

4   Use a quill, mop or rubber to apply the colour as appropriate. Allow a few minutes for the colour to dry before carrying on to the next process.

5   Fasten colour with a coat of polish. On tabletops coat with heat resisting polish and continue to use this polish in following stages. On cheaper work a coat of 50:50 button and amber varnish may be used. Where this is used finish the job using button polish, but never with heat resisting pale polish.

Bodying up

1 Paper down smooth and flat with fine garnet paper using raw linseed oil as a lubricant applied thinly on the paper.
2 Apply a few rubbers of thinned polish in the direction of the grain.
3 Using circular movements followed by smooth figures-of-eight (using a small amount of raw linseed oil as a lubricant), apply a sufficient amount of polish by rubbers to choke the grain as required.
4 To remove the oil, add methylated spirit to the rubber and use straight rubber actions until the work is clean and bright. Then leave it overnight to harden.

Finishing off

1 During the hardening process the polished surface will settle (sink slightly). Using an old piece of 150 grade garnet paper with oil on or a sanding pad, paper the work lightly to remove any slight marks.
2 Repeat the bodying up process until the surface is flat and even (and all the grain is choked if so required).
3 Remove all oil by adding methylated spirit to the rubber as before until the surface is completely clear (i.e. no oil smears remain).

Progress check list

The list below is a quick reference to allow you to see what each stage should have produced.

ACTION	RESULT
STRIPPING	CLEAN
NEUTRALIZING	CLEAN
PAPERING	REPAIRS, FILLED AND FLAT
STAIN	RIGHT COLOUR AND EVEN
FILLER	EVEN, ALL SURPLUS REMOVED
PAPER	EVEN, NO COLOUR BROKEN
1ST COAT (SEAL)	EVEN, NO RUNS
PAPER	SMOOTH, ALL HOLES FILLED
FAD (1ST FEW RUBBERS)	SMOOTH, GOOD RUBBER
COLOUR	NATURAL, CLEAN LOOK
2ND COAT	GOOD, FLAT, EVEN COAT
PAPERING	FLAT, SMOOTH, NO BROKEN COLOUR
BODY-UP	FULL, FLAT, THIN
PAPER	FLAT, EVEN
FINISH	CLEAN, FLAT AND FULL
MATTING	EVEN
WAX	NOT TOO MUCH
DISTRESSING	NATURAL LOOKING

5

*P*OLISHES AND
WHEN TO USE THEM

If you look in the catalogue of a good polish suppliers you will see a bewildering list of polishes, a few of which are listed below:

    black polish
    red polish
    French polish
    *pale amber varnish
    *extra pale polish
    pure button polish
    *pure button polish 4lb
    pure button polish 6lb
    brown sealer
    white sealer
    *heavy white sealer
    heat resisting button polish
    *special button polish
    heat resisting dark polish
    *heat resisting pale polish
    special pale polish

Those polishes marked with an asterisk are the only ones we use and can be used on a wide range of jobs for a number of different reasons.

Heavy white sealer

This contains more sediment than either of the other sealers listed above so it helps to fill the grain better. As brown sealer is coloured it will slightly darken some timbers, so if you are trying to achieve as natural a finish as possible the heavy white sealer is best. Sealer can only be applied once and always with a brush. It should only be applied to bare or stained wood.

Button polish

The term 4lb button polish means that 4lb of shellac has been dissolved in one gallon of methylated spirit to make the polish (approx 2kg of shellac to 5l of methylated spirit). It can be used on any timber though it does tend to slightly alter the colour as it is a warm nutty brown colour. It is traditionally recommended for use on oak, but is suitable for all timbers where a transparent polish is not required. It is sufficiently durable for everyday domestic use and can be used on all items of furniture.

Button polish can be used at all stages after sealing, and even on top of old polish that has been thoroughly prepared (see Chapter 15).

Heat-resisting pale polish

If the item to be polished must be kept as light as possible use this polish at all stages after sealing.

If the item to be polished needs a more durable finish (e.g. table or dressing table tops) use heat-resisting pale polish at the second coating and finishing stages.

Never use 4lb button polish on top of heat-resisting pale polish, though it is perfectly all right to use heat-resisting pale polish on top of button.

Heat-resisting pale polish should not be used on top of old polishes.

Pale amber varnish

This varnish should be used only when mixed in the ratio of 50:50 with 4lb button polish. It is used at the second coating stage on cheaper jobs as it gives a quick build. It should be used only if the underlying polish is button. It must not be used for table tops or in conjunction with heat-resisting pale polish. It is best used on table bases and chairs.

Button polish or special button polish should be used on top of pale amber varnish for the finishing stages.

Special button polish

This is usually used for the finishing stages after a 50:50 mix of button and amber varnish has been second coated on to a job. It gives a quick shine and helps to remove oil at the finishing stages. It should be used only on cheaper work and never on table tops. It should never be used in conjunction with heat-resisting pale polish.

Extra pale polish

This is suitable for using on top of properly prepared old polish where a transparent finish is required. Do not use in conjunction with any other polish.

6

STRIPPING OR CLEANING AND STRIPPING OUT UPHOLSTERY

You first need to assess whether the piece of furniture in front of you requires stripping or merely cleaning down. There will always be controversy as to whether you strip a piece at all, especially if it is old and would not have been French polished originally. We find that much of the furniture we get through our workshop is so bad that it needs stripping and repolishing, and we will French polish pieces that were not previously polished because we can achieve the same result but with superior materials. No doubt we can hear the purists among you screaming in horror, but we think that when a piece of furniture becomes extremely decrepit it needs to be stripped.

The majority of domestic furniture is not worth an enormous amount of money so it will not markedly alter the value of the piece if it is stripped and repolished, but if you have a valuable item and you think it will benefit from cleaning, try that first before you think about stripping it.

Stripping out upholstery

Before stripping away the polish, you should remove any upholstery that is to be replaced. You will need several tools in order to do this:

- a ripping chisel
- a mallet
- a pair of pliers
- a staple remover

When using the ripping chisel to remove upholstery tacks ensure that the piece of furniture is secured – e.g. a loose seat can be cramped to the bench and a chair can be pushed up against a wall. When hitting the ripping chisel aim away from yourself and always remove in the direction of the grain (Fig. 14). If you try to knock out the tacks across the grain you will risk splitting the wood.

Fig 14 Use a ripping chisel and mallet to remove old upholstery. Work in the direction of the grain

If you do not need to remove the upholstery but want to clean or strip the item of furniture, cover up the upholstery using newspaper or polythene held in place with masking tape.

You may need pliers if the tacks break off. If the upholstery you are ripping out has been stapled down the task of getting it out is more troublesome as there are usually a great number of staples and they are difficult to remove. You will need a special staple remover which you should be able to buy at an upholstery suppliers.

If a piece of furniture has been upholstered several times there will be a great number of holes which need filling or the new tacks will not hold in place very well. The best thing to fill such holes with is a mixture of fine sawdust and polyvinyl acetate, or PVA glue. Mix it to a fine paste and apply to the holes with a penknife or spatula. Do not overfill the holes as once the paste hardens it is very difficult to remove any excess.

If the edge over which the upholstery is to be pulled is jagged, it is wise to glue a strip of calico over it. The glue will also help to stop the edge splitting.

For a clean job in which there is no danger of marking the final cover, we proceed as follows: first, we will normally rip out everything (i.e. cover, stuffing and springs etc.) and remove all tacks and staples. We then strip off the polish and carry out any repairs. After we have polished up to but not including the finishing off stage, we take the work to the upholsterer who upholsters up to calico (i.e. the cover before the final cover). We then touch up any necessary marks and finish off the polishing. The upholsterer puts on the final cover and braid.

Cleaning materials and techniques

There are a number of cleaners that you can make very easily and we will list the mildest first **A** and the severest last **G**. Always start with the mildest if you are unsure of the effect the cleaner will have, as it can do no harm and will probably improve the appearance of the piece of furniture.

A Briwax.
B Raw linseed oil and pure turpentine in equal measures.
C Raw linseed oil, pure turpentine and methylated spirit in equal measures.
D Raw linseed oil, pure turpentine, methylated spirit and vinegar in equal measures.
E Raw linseed oil, pure turpentine, methylated spirit, vinegar and warm water in equal measures.
F A small amount of washing soda in hot water.
G A small amount of 0.880 ammonia in hot water.

A should be applied with a piece of towelling to one small area at a time and buffed up vigorously. This is a very good cleaner but takes a lot of effort so do not be tempted to tackle too large an area in one go. You should not French polish over Briwax or any other wax.

B to **E** should be well mixed before use and applied to an area (e.g. one side of a chest of drawers) with a soft cloth or piece of towelling and rubbed up well. Stubborn dirt can be removed with a piece of 0000 grade steel wool gently and evenly rubbed in the direction of the grain without concentrating too much on any one area.

F and **G** should be used when hot. Wear rubber gloves. Use a piece of towelling and rub down one small area at a time, with a piece of grade 0000 steel wool again in reserve for stubborn dirt. On a particularly grimy job scouring powder can be used but take care not to break the surface of the polish. After cleaning down with **F** or **G** neutralize the surface with clean water and then dry it off.

After cleaning down with **B** to **G** the cleaner will need time to dry before the surface is papered down to ensure a smooth surface on which to apply new polish. Rubbering and any necessary colouring can then be done, so refer to Chapter 13 for the next process.

Stripping, materials and techniques

If the polish on the furniture is in a poor condition or the colour needs to be altered substantially it will be necessary to strip off the entire old surface down to the bare wood.

It is essential at this stage to dismantle the piece of furniture so that it will be easy to handle. If, for example, you were to dismantle a gateleg table you would need to place the table face down on the bench using bench pads to protect it. First remove the leaves, making sure you mark which one came from which side, leaving the hinges on the leaves (Fig. 15). Next remove the gates, again marking where they came from. We usually leave the centre top on the table base unless the base needs repairing. If you remove the centre top, again mark it (Figs. 16–17).

We would generally leave the hinges on the leaves so that we can hold onto them when polishing without risking marking the face of the leaf. We will often use the hinges to screw the leaves to the bench so that when polishing they do not move. This also avoids marking or damaging the soft polish as there is no need to hold the polished pieces in place with the hands.

If you are removing or unscrewing fittings from an old piece of furniture it is always best to mark their exact position as very often a fitting was made to fit in one place only; hinges are a prime example of this. When you have removed all the fittings place them in a container and label it clearly.

Fig 15   Marking table leaves before dismantling

Fig 16   The correct way to use a screw driver. All the pressure should come through the shoulder, and having the screwdriver and the arm in line is essential

Fig 17   The hinges remain on the leaf and all the fittings are put into a labelled jar

When you wish to strip only part of a job mask up the areas not to be stripped so that you do not accidentally mark them with stripper (Fig. 18).

We find that methyl chloride stripper is best for stripping paint, polish or varnish. Rubber gloves are essential as the stripper is a severe irritant to the skin. Always use it in a well-ventilated area and avoid splashing it on the skin or into the eyes: if contact occurs with the eyes apply copious amounts of water and seek medical advice. Wash off any splashes on the skin with water to neutralize the stripper.

You will also require a tin to work from, a paint brush for applying stripper, a paint scraper for removing softened polish, grade 3 steel wool, a wire brush and waste paper into which you can put the material (Fig. 19).

When opening a new can of stripper take care, as gas can build up inside, especially in warm weather. First remove the screw cap, then, wrapping a piece of towel round

Fig 18 Masking up the base if you only want to strip the top

Fig 19 All the essentials of a stripper kit

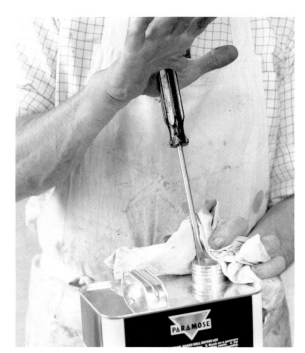

Fig 20 Opening a new can of methyl chloride stripper – note the rag to stop the fumes escaping

a steel screwdriver (preferably stainless steel) or similar sharp tool, place this over the top of the opening and apply pressure to pierce the seal. The towelling will stop any built-up fumes escaping too quickly (Fig. 20).

Pour the stripper into a tin can (do not use plastic as it will rot this and it will etch glass or china) of suitable size (approx. ½l). When pouring stripper out of a new and, therefore, full tin hold it so that the filler cap is at the top, so in effect you pour out over the handle. This stops the stripper pouring unevenly.

Always start by stripping from the top first. Remember: strip **down** and polish **up**. If you wish to strip a chest of drawers start by stripping the top, then one side and half the front, next the other side and the other half of the front, and finally all the drawers together.

Apply a liberal coat of stripper to the area to be stripped and allow it to work for a few minutes; and as it begins to penetrate

Fig 21 Wear rubber gloves and a long-sleeved shirt to protect against stripper splashes. Apply the stripper liberally with an old paint brush

Fig 22 Wait for the polish to bubble before removing

Fig 23 Use a sharp scraper to remove all the material

Fig 24 Scrape off onto a piece of paper which can be disposed of later

the old finish it will start to bubble and craze. If the stripper dries up quickly apply another liberal coat of stripper and allow it to work. When removing the softened finish make sure the surface is still wet – if it has dried it will not be easily removed (Figs. 21–24).

Use a paint scraper of adequate size and

Fig 25 A wire brush can be used to get into grooves and carvings

Fig 26 A moulding scraper can be used on shaped pieces

shape and remove the softened material with swift even movements. This should remove the greatest part of the old finish. Next apply another liberal coat of stripper, remove this by rubbing vigorously with a piece of grade 3 steel wool in the direction of the grain, and pay particular attention to the moulds and carvings (Fig. 27). Never tear steel wool but cut it with an old pair of scissors.

If areas of moulding and carving are difficult to get at you can use a wire brush (Fig. 25). Use a wire brush only on hard woods such as mahogany and oak, and never on pine as it is too soft. It is also useful to have a shaped paint scraper for use on turned work (Fig. 26).

It is not necessary to strip certain areas

- under table leaves
- inside chair frames
- inside cupboards
- the back of cupboard doors

Fig 27 Shape grade 3 steel wool to the job to remove the last traces of old polish

Dealing with these will be covered in Chapter 15.

Fig 28 Neutralize stripper with hot ammonia
water, applied liberally with a piece of
towelling

Fig 29 Use a clean piece of steel wool to remove
last traces of dirt after neutralizing. Shape
the steel wool to get into mouldings

You will next need to neutralize the
stripper so that no residue is left that might
attack any subsequent finishes. You can
use a number of agents:

- a small amount of 0.880 ammonia in
  hot water, a tablespoon in 2.5l (½gal.)
- turpentine substitute
- methylated spirit
- solvent thinners

Apply any of the above with a piece of
towelling to a small area at a time as they
evaporate quite quickly (Fig. 28). Use a
clean piece of steel wool and rub vigorously
in the direction of the grain to leave the
surface clean (Fig. 29).

We prefer to use ammonia water as it is
a mild bleach and helps to remove a lot of
old stains.

However, when neutralizing veneered
furniture we tend to use methylated spirit,
as it is possible when using ammonia
water to get the piece too wet and so risk
softening the underlying glue. Many people
are hesitant about stripping veneered furniture, and some books even say that
stripper must never be used on it. We strip
both veneered and solid furniture very
regularly and do not encounter any problems. It is important with veneered items
to ensure that the stripper has thoroughly
softened the old finish and that when
removing it, you do not dig the scraper into
the veneer and thus risk damaging it.

When you have finished stripping and
neutralizing an item leave it on one side to
dry, preferably overnight.

7

TIMBER
PREPARATION

Fig 30 Chiselling the joint clean ready to apply glue

Fig 31 Hold the chisel steady, sliding it between index finger and thumb to stop it slipping

It is best to carry out any necessary repairs before filling holes or joints as the repair may need filler around it. If a joint is loose, gently use a mallet to knock it apart, taking care to aim your blows as close to the joint as possible as if you hit a rail in the centre it is likely to break the rail and not loosen the joint. Once freed, the joint can be reglued properly.

After taking an item to pieces the joints need cleaning, i.e. all the old glue must be removed, and this is best done with a sharp chisel. Where possible hold the piece in a vice so you have both hands free. When items are too large to be held in a vice place them at a convenient height on the bench and work with care (Fig. 30–31). Remember that a blunt chisel can do more harm than a sharp one.

Note: When reglueing try to assess what the original glue could have been and use one as similar to that as possible; otherwise there might be lack of adhesion.

If you are using animal glue on older jobs it must be hot (not boiling) and should run off the brush without forming drops. Work quickly but ensure that you have used sufficient glue (Figs. 32–33).

Fig 32   Apply animal glue whilst hot – it should run from the brush without forming drops

Fig 33   Ensure you apply sufficient glue

Types of glue

There is a wide range of glues available for use by furniture restorers. These include:

- animal
- fish
- casein
- polyvinyl acetate

Animal glue

This category includes Scotch glue, which is obtained from the skins and bones of animals, though it is best when animal skins alone are used. If bought ready prepared (e.g. Croid Aero), it needs no heat to apply it. However, Scotch glue usually comes as 'pearls', which need to be steeped in water, then heated in a glue pot (never with a naked flame and never to boiling point) and stirred until thoroughly mixed. To test the consistency, raise the brush a few inches above the pot, and the glue should run down freely without breaking up into drops – neither should it be lumpy. The glue should be applied when hot. It is an extremely strong glue that is not liable to stain the wood but be aware that it is not particularly water or heat-resistant.

If the furniture is pre-1940s it is likely to have been glued together with animal glue, so you must use this again. Perished animal glue is normally very brittle and will often fall away into dust; it is honey coloured and smells slightly sweet when broken down.

Fish glue

This is best when made from isinglass, which is extracted from the bladder of the sturgeon. In lower quality glues the heads, skins and cartilage of the fish are used. It normally comes in tubes and is applied cold. Because of its high cost it tends to be used only for small jobs.

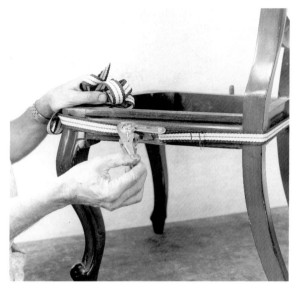

Fig 34 A ratchet webbing (band) cramp is ideal for holding awkward shapes. It can be used to apply a lot of pressure without needing to bother with protective packing pieces

Fig 35 Cramping up a chair with sash cramps – note the use of blocks to protect the wood. Ensure the chair is square before fully tightening

Fig 36 The sash cramps can safely be left in place. Be careful not to walk into the projecting cramps, and always place the cramped piece out of the way until the cramps are ready to remove

Fig 37 All the materials you will need for timber preparation

Casein glue

The base of this glue is skimmed milk. It is precipitated by the addition of a weak acid, and is sold as a light coloured powder. After being mixed with cold water it is used cold, and has the advantage of being very strong and considerably more water-resistant than animal glue. Its disadvantage is that it is liable to stain the wood: especially mahogany, oak and other woods containing a relatively high proportion of acid.

Polyvinyl acetate

A cold setting resin glue in the form of a white and fairly thick liquid, this is used from the container without a hardener. It is a very flexible glue as it can be used not only on wood but on plastics, fabrics and hardboard. It is extremely strong, highly water-resistant and unlikely to stain. Where the furniture to be repaired is more modern this is probably the best glue to use.

Cramps are invaluable when holding a piece together to reglue it. The ratchet webbing cramp, only recently available, is ideal for awkward items (Fig. 34). However, some jobs require the use of more than one cramp at a time so having a wide range is essential. Masking tape is often a good way to hold things together, e.g. for veneers or in small awkward areas.

Note: Always ensure that the item you are cramping up is square and/or flat before leaving it as it will be difficult to adjust once the glue starts to set (Figs. 35–36).

Fillers

As many faults as possible should be corrected at the bare wood stage whether the piece is brand new or stripped. Holes,

joints and faults should all be filled where necessary. The materials used to fill at this stage are:

- epoxy resin filler (e.g. Timberfill – similar to car body filler but it comes coloured in various shades)
- water or cellulose-based plastic filler (e.g. Brummer or Quirk-O, which is available in a range of colours)
- shellac sticks (beaumontage)

Epoxy resin filler

Bought complete with a tube of hardener, this is particularly useful on large holes, timber splits, edges and corners. If the area to be filled is large, build up the filler in layers, allowing each layer to harden before the next is applied.

Epoxy resin filler is moderately expensive and wasteful in use as it is difficult to mix the exact amount required. It hardens very quickly when mixed so it should be used within about five minutes – therefore, do not mix too much at a time. Do not overfill holes as epoxy filler does not shrink on drying and it is very hard to sand. It should be ready to sand within a couple of hours.

Epoxy resin does not take stain and is a solid colour. Therefore, use a filler slightly lighter than the finished colour required and it can then be coloured at a later stage (see Chapter 13).

Note: It is best applied with a blunt penknife (a smoker's knife is ideal) as the blade is rounded and not sharp (Fig. 38).

Plastic filler

This is suitable for filling pin and worm holes, bruises that cannot be steamed out and smaller joints. It will shrink on drying

Fig 38 Filling a corner with epoxy resin filler. Do not mix too much as it hardens quickly

Fig 39 Small splits can be filled with a plastic filler. A blunt penknife is ideal for the job

so it needs to be left slightly proud. It takes longer to dry than Epoxy filler so should be left for a couple of hours at least, or better still overnight.

It has the advantage of being relatively cheap. It is best bought in tins because if it dries up (e.g. if the lid has been left off) the relevant solvent can be stirred in to soften it and it is ready for use again. With Quirk-O water is added to soften it. Note that plastic filler is not suitable for use on corners or edges as it would knock out easily, and is best applied with a blunt penknife (Fig. 39).

Shellac sticks (beaumontage)

A shellac stick is a mixture of shellac resin and colour made into a convenient stick, which needs to be melted into the hole and sets very rapidly. It is easy to melt too much beaumontage and this leaves a mound which needs to be chiselled off. Shellac sticks are less convenient to use than plastic filler and we no longer use

them, but they are still available from specialist stores.

Papering down (sanding)

After all repairs have been carried out and all holes filled, it is necessary to paper the timber in order to remove any remaining faults (e.g. shallow scratches) and to obtain a smooth surface ready for staining. However, note that in order for the stain to penetrate the wood the surface must not be overpapered; i.e. if the surface is papered so that all the fibres in the timber are flat (such that it feels as smooth as glass) the stain will have little chance of penetrating and the subsequent overlying polish will have a poor key.

If faults are not removed at this stage they will be emphasized when polish is applied, so take your time. Some scratches and marks may best be removed by using a cabinet scraper first and then papering. Marks such as ink stains will be dealt with in Chapter 8.

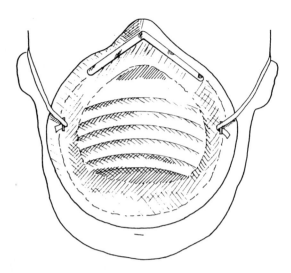

Fig 40 A disposable dust mask should be worn when preparing bare wood. Masks are not required when using stripper or polish but it is always advisable to work in a well-ventilated area

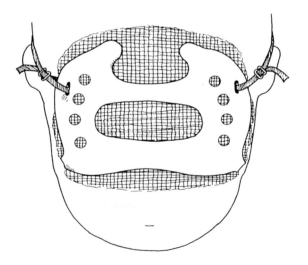

Fig 41 A two-piece dust mask is also available. The light metal plate holds replaceable pads, and this should also be used when papering timber

The method of smoothing wood traditionally was with glass paper or sand paper. Modern papers in use are garnet, silicon carbide and sanding pads. The earlier papers made of sand or glass grit were glued to a thick paper backing. Modern abrasive grits are fixed to a much finer backing paper which makes the paper more flexible. The standard size of paper is 230 × 280mm (11 × 9in). Papers are graded by the amount of grit (be it garnet or glass) per linear inch.

When papering any timber it is wise to use a dust mask as the dust produced is very fine. The dust from rosewood is probably the most dangerous and is also noxious. The most convenient masks to use are the lightweight disposable one piece ones (Fig. 40). Other types include two piece masks with replaceable filters (Fig. 41). The choice of mask will depend on how much sanding you are liable to be doing. It is also best to try to work in a well-ventilated area or to use an extractor fan to remove the dust.

Garnet paper

This is of two sorts, either finishing paper or cabinet paper. The former has a thinner and more flexible backing paper. We find that finishing paper is best suited to our needs as we often need to fold the paper when sanding. We use garnet papers in a range of grades from 80 (the coarsest we require) to 150 (the finest we require).

Silicon carbide paper

This paper is for use with modern lacquers and polyurethanes, and is also very good for cleaning up metal. It has an exceedingly hard and durable grit but we do not recommend using it for papering bare wood or French polish as it actually cuts the surface of the polish. We use it mostly for cleaning dirty brass.

Sanding pads

Very new on the market, these are made from thin polyurethane foam with silicon carbide grit glued to both sides (see List of Suppliers). They come in fine and coarse grades and are very useful when sanding turnings. We now use them a great deal instead of garnet paper when papering polish. We do not use them on bare wood as they do not have a sharp enough cutting edge. Despite our comments above we have found that on these sanding pads the silicon carbide abrades the polish, but does **not** cut it.

Fig 43   When sanding by hand hold the paper firmly and keep the hand flat

Using garnet paper

When we use garnet paper we tear it in half along its width, giving us a piece 230 × 140mm (9 × 5½in). We then fold the half

Fig 44   Shape the garnet paper around the mould

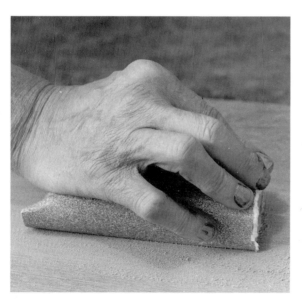

Fig 42   Wrap the garnet paper round the cork block. The heel of the hand applies pressure

sheet into thirds – in this way the grit on the inside fold holds the face side firmly and prevents the paper tearing.

When papering flat areas a sanding (cork) block must be used in order to obtain a flat surface. Simply wrap the paper round the block in the most convenient manner. Apply plenty of pressure ensuring that the heel of your hand is pushing down on the back of the cork block and that you are using the upper arm muscles (Fig. 42). Always paper in the direction of the grain, keeping the strokes as parallel to the grain as possible. When sanding veneers such as burr walnut choose one direction to sand in and maintain it as you sand with progressively finer paper.

If you are papering a large area do half of it at a time so that you do not need to stretch too far to reach the other half, as overstretching does not allow you to exert full and even pressure.

Moulds and small areas are best sanded by hand but make sure that you keep your hands flat and the pressure even (Figs. 43–44). If you sand a large area by hand there is a tendency to leave ridges where uneven pressure has been applied.

Start papering with the coarsest paper first (i.e. grade 80) then move down through the grades to finish with a fine paper. On most timbers the finishing grade should be 120 grit but on fine veneers, especially figured ones, you need to finish off with 150 grit.

Ensure that there are no sharp edges, especially if you are preparing a new piece of furniture. Round the edges off slightly, otherwise the subsequent stain and polish will wear off quickly as the edges become rounded naturally.

Bruises

Shallow bruises can often be taken out by using a hot iron and a damp rag. Place the damp rag over the bruise and rub the iron locally over it. This will cause the fibres to swell and may remove the bruise.

8

*B*LEACHING, LIMING
AND DISTRESSING

Bleaching

Bleaching is done for one of two reasons:

- to lighten wood
- to remove marks such as ink or iron

Types of bleach

There are two main types of bleach and they are:

- ones that consist of two solutions, often called A and B or 1 and 2 bleach
- ones that will work without the action of a second agent

Two pack bleaches The number 1 or A solution is alkaline, usually dilute ammonia or dilute caustic potash, while the number 2 or B solution is normally a high percentage hydrogen peroxide.

The alkaline is applied first and tends to darken the wood. After about five minutes the number 2 or B solution is applied. The two chemicals then react to do the bleaching.

There are custom-made two pack bleaches available but it is quite easy to make your own. Number 1 or A is made from 1 part 0.880 ammonia and 5 parts

Fig 45 When removing an ink stain with bleach (the best being oxalic acid) wear rubber gloves and use a piece of towelling to apply it. Apply the bleach to the area of the stain very liberally and allow it to dry naturally – the mark will fade as the bleach dries. If the mark has not been removed by one application keep applying it until it is no longer obvious. After the mark has been removed it is wise to bleach the whole area around it to ensure you are not left with a very light patch. Once all bleaching has been carried out the area should be wiped down with clean water to ensure that all traces of bleach have been removed

water. Number 2 or B is made from 1 part 100 volume hydrogen peroxide and two parts water.

Single agent bleaches The best one we have used is oxalic acid. It is bought as fine crystals and needs to be dissolved in hot water before use. It is effective at lightening wood and removing ink marks. Care should be taken when using oxalic acid, however, as it is poisonous.

How to use bleaches

Always be sure to wear rubber gloves when handling either type of bleach and use it in a well-ventilated area (Fig. 45). The traditional method of applying bleach was with a grass brush but we find that a piece of towelling is ideal and has the advantage that it can be disposed of carefully after use.

Do not work out of metal containers as bleach will rot them – glass or stout plastic is fine. Do not use the bleach container for any other substance. Do not store unused mixed bleach as it will rapidly deteriorate. It should always be mixed fresh for the best results.

When the surface of the wood is dry you will be able to see how much effect the bleach has had. Repeat the process if required. Once you have achieved the desired amount of bleaching, wipe the surface down with warm water or methylated spirit to remove any chemical residue.

With experience you will find that ash, beech and elm will bleach easily with one application, while mahogany, oak and walnut require more than one application. Woods such as ebony, rosewood, cherry or satinwood bleach with difficulty or not at all.

If you are trying to bleach out an ink or iron stain it is more effective to place a suitable size piece of towelling over the mark and thoroughly wet it with bleach. Leave it on for as long as possible, ideally overnight. After bleaching a mark it is generally best to bleach the whole area around it. For very stubborn ink or iron marks you can use nitric acid, but take great care in its handling. Make sure the surface is properly neutralized with warm water if you have already tried removing the stain with an alkaline solution (e.g. two pack bleach).

Polishing after bleaching

After bleaching it is best if you seal with heavy white sealer and then polish with heat resisting pale polish in order to keep it as light as possible.

Liming

Among the special finishes currently in use liming is probably the most popular, though it is only really effective on oak as it is an open-grained timber. In order to lime a piece of wood the grain pores must be open so that the liming paste can be rubbed into them.

If you wish to lime a piece of furniture that has been previously polished, you should ensure that it is as clean as possible, bleaching it if it is not light enough (see above). Liming looks most effective where the timber is light in colour. The most popular use of liming currently is in fitted kitchens and bedrooms.

How to lime

Once you have prepared the timber by stripping (if necessary) and papering, open up the grain with a wire brush (Fig. 46).

Fig 46   (top right) Use a firm wire brush to open up the grain of oak before liming. Always use the brush in the direction of the grain and apply a fair amount of pressure, and do not be too hesitant as the more open the grain the better the results

Fig 47   (middle right) Wear rubber gloves and use towelling to apply the liming paste. Apply to a suitable size area, e.g. a kitchen door front. Rub into the grain by going round in circles then rub across the grain

Fig 48   (bottom right) With a clean piece of cloth wipe off the excess grain filler. First rub off across the grain then finish by rubbing off in the direction of the grain

You can rub quite vigorously in the direction of the grain, but take care not to go across the grain as the marks will be severe.

We use a proprietary liming paste. As with grain filling (see Chapter 9) you should not tackle too large an area at a time as the liming paste dries quite quickly. Select the area you wish to lime, and remember to work upwards if you are tackling a piece of furniture and not just a kitchen door. Wear rubber gloves and use a piece of towelling to apply the liming paste, rubbing it firmly into the grain in circular movements and ensuring that all the grain pores are filled (Fig. 47). With a clean piece of towelling rub vigorously and quickly across the grain to remove excess paste (Fig. 48); and last of all, rub in the direction of the grain.

If the item you are liming has moulds or internal corners make sure that there is no build-up of the paste in these areas. The best way to remove it is to take a blunt piece of wood and pick it out. A metal implement tends to mark the surface.

Once the paste has dried (the time taken may vary from manufacturer to manufacturer so read the instructions), very lightly paper the surface to ensure it is flat and to remove any ridges on the surface that should not be there. Take care not to paper through the paste.

Seal with a coat of heavy white sealer. Polish throughout with heat resisting pale polish so that the liming paste is not discoloured and it is kept as light as possible. If any colouring is required it is best to use titanium white pigment only.

Distressing

People wish to make a new piece of furniture look old for two main reasons:

- to distress a new piece of furniture so that it matches in with existing pieces – quite acceptable to us and a technique we often carry out
- to distress a piece to the extent that it becomes a fake – to our way of thinking unethical. For example, some time ago a customer acquired a set of walnut Victorian chairs which she had been told were all genuine. But, on reupholstering, it turned out that two of the chairs were new

How to distress

Remember that the border line between distressing and destroying is fine, and that with a new piece of furniture this is best done at the bare wood stage (Fig. 49).

The tools needed are:

- a rasp
- a round piece of hard wood or metal rod
- a scraper
- a canvas bag with smooth pebbles in
- garnet paper

Fig 49 Distressing should not be excessive. Stain can be used to shade an area to give it a worn look. Ink or water stains in small numbers will look effective. Avoid making too many scratches and/or dents. A well-distressed item can look very pleasing but there is a fine line between distressing and destroying

Fig 50 Shading can look effective on the right piece of furniture. Ensure that the line between the light and dark stain is gradual so that it looks more natural

Fig 51 Distressing can be achieved by shading to make the item look worn. You would expect a tabletop, for example, to be darker at the edges. Apply the lighter stain all over the job then with a darker stain apply to the edges. Then gently wipe over with a clean cloth so that the edge of the darker stain is not obvious. The colours should merge gradually

You need to think carefully about the extent to which you wish to distress.

Remember that on an old piece you will not have sharp edges. Rails of tables and chairs will be worn. Bottoms of legs will be rubbed and knocked. Tops of tables and chests will have marks, e.g. ink spills and circles from metal containers.

The bag of pebbles and the metal or wooden rod are used by quite literally hitting the piece of furniture with them. Do not be too violent and think carefully about the number and location of the indentations they will produce. The rasp and scraper can be used to take off edges. Again, be cautious in their use.

After you have distressed the wood sufficiently you need to make a decision on the colour required. If you are using a water stain you need to put it on unevenly to represent exposure to light and wear. Two ways of doing this are:

- Stain the job all over and let it dry, then take a piece of 120 grade garnet paper and artistically break the colour by removing the stain to simulate wear and tear.
- Using a medium-coloured water stain apply all over, then use a darker stain over the parts which would not have been worn. By rubbing with a piece of towelling damp with water, the stains can be blended so a solid line will not be seen (Figs 50–51).

For an oil-based stain you can use a similar technique but use turpentine substitute instead of water to get the shaded effect.

When dry apply a thin coat of heavy white sealer; when this is dry it is time to paper down. Remember now that papering can be done unevenly – you can rub some edges deliberately to remove stain and simulate wear, and can leave small imperfections unfilled.

Now apply a few thin rubbers of button polish and roughly assemble the job. With

Fig 52 Distressing can be done by imitating old
worm holes. This is done by colouring, i.e.
coating dark colour with a quill in small
hole- or line-like marks. This gives the
impression of old worm holes that have
been filled up by years of applying wax

artistic colouring the whole work should
now be blended to the required effect.
Second coat with thin button polish to
avoid getting too high a shine. When the
polish is hard gently paper with an old
piece of oiled 150 grade garnet paper to
avoid scratches and apply two or three
rubbers of thin polish. If required, you can
wax the work the following day, then
abrade it with fine steel wool to tone the
surface down.

Distressing is a particularly interesting
procedure as the effects obtained are
relative to the skill and knowledge of the
restorer. One special technique is that of
simulatry worm holes to imitate ageing
and wear and tear. This can be done at
either the timber preparation stage or the
colouring stage.

At the timber preparation stage – use a
nail punch and a hammer. Do not choose
a punch with a large diameter or the holes
will look unnatural (a medium sized panel
pin is also suitable for this purpose).
Carefully make a few small holes, fairly
close together in an appropriate location e.g. the base of a table or chair
leg or close to a glue joint which is
where such holes would naturally occur.
These, when stained, become small black
holes and are easily mistaken for worm
holes.

At the colouring stage – in order to
simulate worm holes at the colouring stage
all you will need is a swan's quill and
some dark colour (black and very dark).
Using the quill, artistically 'paint-in' holes
with the colour in any appropriate area.
Longer lines can be painted-in to imitate
a surface which over the years has been
worn away to expose the pathway of the
worm (Fig. 52).

9

STAINS AND GRAIN FILLERS

The object of staining is both to bring out the natural beauty of the grain, and to alter the colour of the wood so that the piece of furniture approaches the final colour required. There will be variations in shade among pieces of wood on the same item, depending upon their position; i.e. vertical timbers will look different from horizontal ones (Fig. 53). When staining, therefore, we have to aim for a general overall colour.

Home woodworkers must give careful thought as to how they would like the finished piece of furniture to look. Some timbers are, of course, chosen for their natural colour and so staining is not required. The current trend seems to be in favour of natural colours where the beauty of the wood is enhanced.

Some woods such as beech, chestnut, teak and all fruit woods do not stain well and are best left in their natural colour. It is, therefore, advisable to spend some time considering the timber you wish to use and the colour you wish it to be.

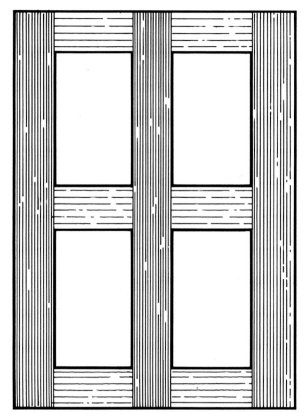

Fig 53 Vertical and horizontal timbers will vary on the same job. Horizontals will look lighter. If the piece was turned through 90° the horizontals would look darker because they have, in effect, become the verticals

Stains

The choice of stains is really very extensive, and bewildering, and ranges from a 1906 recipe made from old beer that has

Fig 54 A selection of materials used when staining. Note the tin containers for stains and the plastic one for pure turpentine

had nails soaking in it for two weeks, to the more modern, light fast stains most commonly used in industry (Fig. 54).

Stains fall into 4 groups:

- chemical
- oil
- water
- spirit

Chemical stains

With these there is a chemical reaction between the stain and certain woods. There are basically three chemical stains that we use today, namely:

- fuming
- bichromate of potash
- raw linseed oil and pure turpentine

Fuming This method of staining is generally only suitable for use on oak, turning white oak a grey weathered colour. It can also be used on walnut and mahogany which turn slighly brown. Fuming is achieved by standing the furniture to be stained in an airtight box, tent or room and placing small bowls of 0.880 ammonia around the piece. The fumes given off affect the tannin in the timber, thus altering its shade. This method was discovered in stables, when it was found that the oak beams used in stables altered colour – it was the ammonia given off in horse urine that did it.

Advantages:

- it is inexpensive

Disadvantages:

- the fumes are noxious
- the colour obtained is variable and will depend upon the length of time it is subjected to the fumes and the amount of ammonia used. Thus it is not possible to match colours by staining in this way as there are too many variables

Bichromate of potash This stain consists of crystals which must be mixed with hot water and in application needs to be treated as water stains. However, the results are variable as bichromate will only stain certain woods due to the nature of the chemical reaction between the stain and the wood. It is most suitable for use on mahogany, turning it a red colour. The depth of colour will depend on how strongly the stain was mixed. This stain is ideally suited to use on inlaid mahogany as it will only darken the mahogany and not effect the inlay.

Advantages:

- it is inexpensive
- it can be used on inlaid furniture

Disadvantages:

- it raises the grain

- it is slow drying (approximately 24 hours)
- the colour it produces will vary depending on the strength of the mixture, so it is not possible to match different items of furniture of different timber
- the final colour cannot be seen until polish has been applied
- new timber must be dampened first to raise the grain and then papered before staining; after staining it must be papered again

Raw linseed oil and pure turpentine This is a stain you are unlikely to read about elsewhere and it is one we use a great deal. It consists of equal parts of raw linseed oil and pure turpentine. We use it on mahogany, walnut, rosewood and very old oak. It darkens the wood whilst enhancing the grain, giving it great clarity when polished. It needs to be applied with a piece of towelling and then left to dry for 24 hours. As with bichromate it can be used on inlaid furniture as it does not affect the inlay.

Advantages:

- it produces a beautiful colour and gives great clarity of grain
- it is inexpensive to use
- it can be used to stain inlaid work without affecting them

Disadvantages:

- it must be left to dry for 24 hours at least
- it will not be possible to stain different timbers to the same colour as it affects them differently

Despite these drawbacks we would strongly recommend its use on the appropriate timbers and you will be spoilt for using anything else (Fig. 55).

Fig 55   When a table top is stained with raw linseed oil and pure turpentine the inlay is not stained and the grain is kept clear

Oil stains

These are oil-soluble dyes dissolved in turpentine, naphtha or similar oils. They come in a wide range of colours and will vary from manufacturer to manufacturer, so it is best to get used to one range of colours. They can be intermixed to obtain a wide range of colours. We stock only five colours, which are:

- brown mahogany
- rosewood
- golden oak
- dark oak
- black

Oil stains should be poured into an old tin container for working from; do not use plastic as they will rot it and glass will be etched.

They are applied using either towelling or a brush as appropriate and rubber gloves should be worn (Figs. 56–57).

Fig 56 A good quality paint brush is ideal for getting into awkward corners

Advantages:

- they do not raise the grain
- they are relatively inexpensive
- they are relatively fast drying (approximately 4 hours)
- the colour you see when first applied is the colour you will get
- they are easy to apply and where the stain is overlapped there is no build-up of colour
- they are non-pigmented stains so they do not obliterate the grain
- they can be intermixed to obtain a wide range of colours

We use these stains widely as we find them very flexible and easy to use.

Water stains

Water stains in one form or another have been in use for centuries. They are usually obtained as crystals dissolved in boiling water to obtain a required colour. The most widely used are Vandyke brown crystals and Mahogany crystals. A water stain can be almost anything that will dissolve in water, e.g. coffee or beer, so if you had the time you could experiment to get some interesting results.

When using water-based stains on new wood first wet the surface thoroughly to raise the grain, and after leaving overnight, paper it smooth, and then apply the stain. When this is dry you must paper down again, taking care not to paper through the stain. A piece of old 150 grit garnet paper will be suitable here.

On items that are to be repolished there is no need to raise the grain before staining as the stripping process (and more especially the neutralizing process if ammonia water has been used) will already have done this. When staining a large number of items it is essential to mix sufficient stain as it is very difficult to mix another batch of stain to exactly the same colour. Use towelling to apply the stain and wear rubber gloves.

Advantages:

- they penetrate the timber well
- they are inexpensive to use
- they can produce some good colours

Disadvantages:

- being water-based they need to be left overnight to dry
- they will raise the grain and thus the piece will require sanding after drying
- the final colour is not obvious until polish has been applied, so if you are trying to match stain to the colour of another piece of furniture it will take much time and experimentation

Spirit stains

These stains are widely used in manufacturing as they are very fast drying and are best applied by spray application. Unfortunately they are often sold to the amateur, but should be avoided as they have a tendency to create more problems than they solve.

Advantages:

- they are fast-drying (approximately one hour)
- they are light-fast, i.e. they do not fade too rapidly

Disadvantages:

- because they are fast-drying they cause problems of overlapping, i.e. if you stain one area twice it will be darker than where it was only stained once. This will look unsightly at joints where it is difficult to avoid overlaps
- because they are fast-drying they must be applied quickly which may present a problem on a large item
- they are more expensive than all the other stains
- if you were to brush French polish on over the stain, the polish would soften the stain and so lift some of it, which may result in a streaky appearance. This occurs because the stain and polish share the same solvent, methylated spirit.

Grain fillers

The purpose of a grain filler is to choke the grain, thus saving time and polish; because if grain filler is not used the grain must be filled by polish at the bodying up stage.

We use a thixotropic filler, which is available in a variety of shades, though a clear filler can be bought and pigments mixed in to achieve the required colour.

Only ever use a grain filler **after** staining. If you were to grain fill first the stain would not be able to penetrate into the timber, so

Fig 57 An old piece of towelling can be used to stain large areas. Apply liberally and wipe of excess stain with a clean rag in the direction of the grain

achieve the colour you require with stain first. It is best to choose a grain filler that is slightly darker than the stained colour as it will make the grain stand out to beneficial effect.

After the stain is dry you can grain fill, but do not try to tackle too large an area at a time as the filler dries very quickly. We find that old net curtaining or hessian are the best materials to use to apply it, but towelling will do. First, rub in the filler in circular movements so that you rub across the grain, making sure you push it into the grain (Fig. 58). Then rub in straight movements across the grain to remove the excess (Fig. 59). Taking a clean piece of curtaining rub across the grain, and finally, in the direction of the grain, making sure that you remove all excess filler. Allow it to dry for a couple of hours and then lightly paper with an old piece of 150 grit garnet paper to remove any remaining excess and to obtain a flat surface.

We use grain filler predominantly on large table tops.

 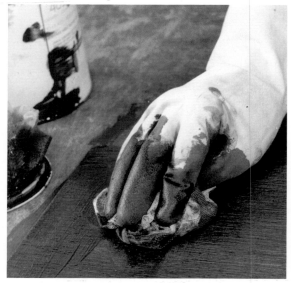

Fig 58   Apply grain filler by rubbing in circles, pushing it into the grain

Fig 59   Remove excess grain filler by first rubbing across the grain and then in the same direction as it

PART TWO
FRENCH POLISHING

10

B RUSHES AND THEIR USES

There are several types of brush that can be used when restoring furniture, namely:

Old paint brushes   These can be used for applying stripper. Have a range of sizes to suit all jobs.

Glue brush   This is essential for use with animal glue.

Selection of brushes for stain   Of use but not essential. Choose only reasonable quality paint or artist's brushes as the stain will rot them eventually.

Wire brush   For use when stripping, especially on turnings or carvings. Take care when using them as they can badly damage the timber if used incorrectly. Use only on hardwood such as mahogany or oak. A wire brush can also be used on oak to open up the grain prior to liming (see Chapter 8).

Grass brush   Traditionally used to apply bleach, but today we would apply bleach with a piece of towelling. The brush was made of special fibre held together with wire which also formed the handle. (It was made of wire, not wood, as bleach does not rot metal as quickly as wood.)

Dust brush A moderate-to-soft long bristled brush with a wooden handle used to remove dust from a sanded job, particularly good at getting at dust lodged in corners and carvings.

Dulling brush Like a good quality shoebrush, and used for dulling a polished surface that is too bright. It can be used in conjunction with pumice powder (see Chapter 18).

Polishing brushes or mops Used for applying sealer and polish and must be looked after carefully.

Polishing mops

Polishing mops have traditionally been made of hog, squirrel or bear hair but within the last few years a different type of hair has been introduced – South American skunk hair or Zorino (Figs 60–61). We find these Zorino mops to be superior in use as

Fig 61 A selection of Zorino mops and swan's quills

the squirrel hair mops are too soft and bear hair mops are too rigid. Zorino mops come in a range of sizes from a number 6 (the smallest) to a number 18 (which is very large indeed).

We also use goose and swan's quills in the colouring process and for touching up. The bristles are bound into a quill so they resemble small brushes, more like artists' brushes, but with short handles.

If you are using a Zorino mop to apply cellulose or Copal varnish, you must keep the brushes separate as the solvents used are incompatible with French polish – i.e. use a separate brush for each type of finish used.

A reasonable kit should consist of:

- For colouring – 2 goose or swan's quills
  - number 6 Zorino mop
  - number 8 Zorino mop
- For coating – number 10 Zorino mop
  - number 12 Zorino mop

Before regular use the brushes need to be 'trained'. To do this soak the brush, completely covering the bristles, in a jar of button polish and leave for about an hour. Remove excess polish from the brush by

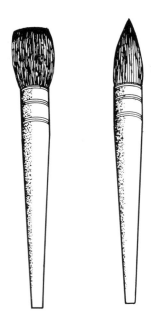

Fig 60 A Zorino mop should be of a chisel shape with all the bristles together

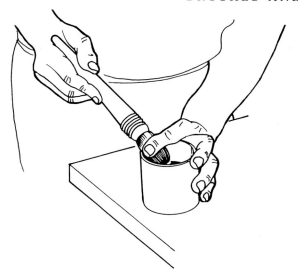

Fig 62 When removing excess polish from a Zorino mop hold it against the side of the container, apply pressure with the index finger and withdraw the brush gently

Fig 63 Remove excess polish by holding the brush against the side of the container with the index finger and withdraw the brush

holding the brush against the side of the polish container with the index finger, and then gently withdraw the brush whilst applying gentle pressure with the finger (Figs 62–3). Then shape the bristles to look like a flat chisel and allow the brush to go hard. Repeat this process about four times over four days, by which time all the bristles in the stock will be held firmly in place and ready for use without any loss of bristles.

When you are about to use a brush, you must soften it up in advance by standing it in methylated spirit or polish. The time required to soften the brush will depend on how long it is since it was last used. Never force the bristles apart if in a hurry to soften the brush, as this will ruin them; and do not leave brushes standing in pots overnight as they will lose their shape.

The brushes do not need to be cleaned each time after use as this tends to remove the body of polish that has formed at the stock and is holding the bristles in place. If the brush has been used for colour simply swill the brush in some clean methylated spirit and then reshape.

If you treat your brushes well they will give you years of service.

11

SEALING

Now that all stripping and timber preparation has been done you can get down to the bit you have been waiting for, namely **French polishing**. Just remember not to rush at polishing and if you make a mess of it put it on one side for a day and then come back to it. It is basically a straight-forward job that requires a lot of practice to get it right, but you can produce very good results first time if you stick to the sequence of actions laid out in this book. See Chapter 4 for the quick guide.

When the stain and/or grain filler has dried you can begin to apply the polish. We first apply a coat of heavy white sealer which is shellac-based. This sealer can, in some cases, be used in place of grain filler as it contains a sediment that helps to fill the grain. It can also be used over grain filler as it will only help to ensure that the grain is choked.

The sealer must be shaken well before use as the sediment will settle to the bottom of its container. It needs to be applied with a brush – we use Zorino mops which are expensive but if looked after properly will last you a long time. See Chapter 10 on how to look after brushes.

The sealer should be poured into a glass or china container for working from, never

Fig 64 Always coat in the direction of the grain whether the area is small or large

Fig 65 When coating turnings hold the brush lightly at the end and flick it gently, thus avoiding getting the turnings too wet

tin or plastic. An old straight-sided cup or mug is ideal. When coating there are several points to note which apply to both sealing and second coating:

Turn the work piece Anti-clockwise if you are right-handed and clockwise if you are left-handed. This ensures that you will be able to hold on to a part of the job that is dry, thus avoiding marking it.

Coat from the bottom upwards If for example you are coating a small table, stand it on the workbench on its feet and coat all the base in the appropriate direction. You will be able to hold on to the top to steady it whilst coating the base. Then place the table on the floor and coat the top, and you should not need to hold the base, thus avoiding marking any of the table.

Coat in the direction of the grain Never across it (Fig. 64).

When coating turnings Hold the mop lightly at the end and flick the polish on; in this circumstance it is often necessary to go across the grain but this is the only occasion when you can do so (Fig. 65).

Never apply too thick a coat But ensure it is even. Once you have coated an area do not go back to try to fill in a small area you have missed; it is best left as you will catch up with it at a later stage.

Coating a large area

When coating a large area (e.g. a dining table top) always follow these simple rules:

Always coat edges first Do not allow any polish on the face of the work, and if you do get polish on the face wipe it off immediately with the side of your hand.

On each brush application Coat the full

width or length of the work piece (depending on the direction of the grain).

Start coating at the edge closest to you Stand so that the grain runs left to right across your body.

Never come on at an edge Visualize a strip of about 100mm (4in) running left to right at the edge closest to you and apply polish in the centre of this strip then brush out to each side, coming *off* centre at the edge. You should now have coated across the full width/length in a strip about 100mm (4in) wide.

Recharge your brush Again imagine a strip of about 100mm (4in), leaving a gap of about 100mm (4in) between the coated strip and the strip to be coated. Coat the second strip, again starting in the middle and working to the edges, at the same time filling in the gap you have left. By coating in this way you will always keep a 'wet edge' to coat up to, thus avoiding ridges. Work in this series of blanks and strips until you have coated the whole piece.

Work swiftly and evenly Never go back to a strip if you have missed a small area; this will only result in pulling up the polish unevenly.

The sealer will dry relatively quickly (about fifteen minutes) as it is soaking

Fig 66   When using a sanding pad it can be shaped to the piece being smoothed

directly into the timber, after which it can be papered smooth. The sealer when dry will feel slightly rough and you are aiming to get this to feel smooth, but you must take care not to paper through the sealer and/or the stain.

We would normally use an old piece of 120 grit garnet paper or one of the newly available sanding pads (Fig. 66). Do not use a cork block, and keep your hands as flat as possible to the workpiece. Avoid creating ridges by pressing too hard with any one finger.

12

R UBBERS AND RUBBERING

A rubber is a piece of apparatus which allows the polisher to apply a thin film of polish to the timber. It is made from polishers' wadding and cotton cloth. The polish is held in the wadding and it flows through the cloth – the more open the cloth the more polish will flow through. Pressure is applied by the index and second finger, and the greater the pressure the greater the amount of polish that will be deposited on the work piece. Throughout rubbering it is the correct combination of pressure and cloth which give the desired results.

If you have read older books you will come across 'fads'; these are merely rubbers without the cloth. They were used to apply the 'sealer coat' of polish. Their use has been superseded by a brush coat of heavy white sealer. A fad today refers to a newly-made rubber with a very open cloth. Fadding serves the purpose of getting thin button polish on to the workpiece quickly, as the open cloth allows a reasonable amount of polish through. If the rag were not used there would be the tendency to get bits of wadding on the job.

The ability to make a rubber and to maintain it during use is most important if you are to succeed in French polishing. It is seemingly very easy to make but in fact takes much practice. Do not be put off though, because if you make and maintain a good rubber it will make the rest of polishing seem easy.

How to make a rubber

Use polishers' wadding and not cotton wool or upholsterers' wadding which are both unsuitable. Be sure to use only a cotton cloth free of linters, avoiding any cloth that is not pure cotton even if it only contains a small percentage of another fibre, as it does not allow the polish to flow through freely and makes the face of the rubber slimy. An open cloth, e.g. cheese cloth, is suitable for the early stages of polishing and a more closely woven one is better for the finishing stages. Bedding or handkerchiefs are usually a good source of polishing cloth.

    The following diagrams (Figs. 67–80) show the stages that need to be followed to make a rubber.

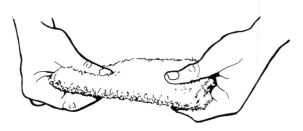

Fig 68   Fold into an oblong of about 100 × 65mm (4 × 2½in)

Fig 69   Form a point with the wadding so that it resembles a half pear shape

Fig 70   Hold the rear of the wadding with the thumb and first two fingers of the right hand

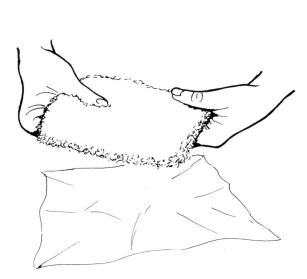

Fig 67   Take a piece of polisher's wadding approximately 200 × 130mm (8 × 5in) long

Fig 71 Totally immerse the wadding in thinned polish. Squeeze out about 50 per cent so that the wadding holds the shape of the half pear

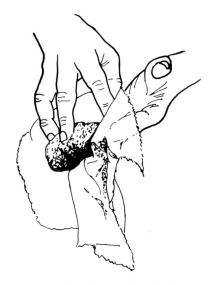

Fig 73 Lay wadding flat on the cloth

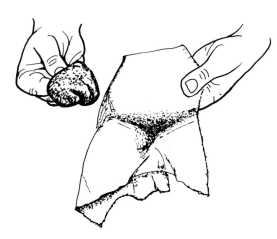

Fig 72 Hold a piece of lint free cloth on the palm of the left hand, hold the wadding in the right hand by the thumb and first two fingers

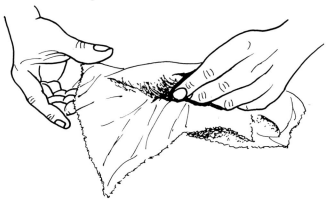

Fig 74 Hold wadding firmly through cloth with thumb and first two fingers of the left hand at the rear

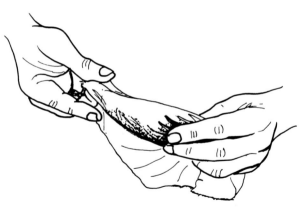

Fig 75 Gently drape cloth over the point of the 'rubber' with thumb and first two fingers of the right hand

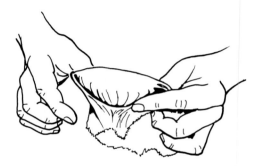

Fig 78 Hold the rubber firmly in the left hand

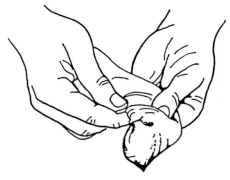

Fig 79 Take up loose cloth and twist from right to left

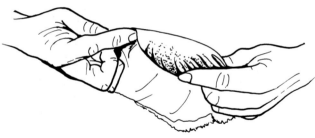

Fig 76 Place the index finger of the right hand under the point and take the cloth past the point, then remove the index finger

Fig 80 The cloth should be twisted tightly upon itself and on top of the rubber

How to hold a rubber

It is important that you learn to hold a rubber correctly as it will make polishing a lot easier. The important points to note about holding a rubber are:

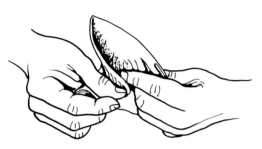

Fig 77 Take up the surplus cloth with the first two fingers of the left hand

The thumb **Do not apply pressure with your thumb** You, along with all other students new to polishing, will fall into the trap of distorting the rubber with your thumb. The result is a rubber with a reduced surface area through which the polish can flow. The thumb's function when holding a rubber is to guide and steady it. You will need to make a conscious effort not to apply pressure, but after a while it will become second nature.

The index and second finger These are placed at the front of the rubber and guide it into awkward areas (Figs. 81–84). Sometimes you will find that you need to place only the index finger at the front, especially if getting into narrow turnings or areas where there is physically no room for both fingers. These fingers also apply pressure downwards and push the polish out of the rubber through the base.

The fourth and small finger These are tucked into the palm and serve to guide and steady the rubber, and to hold the tail in place, stopping it from unwinding or trailing down on to the work piece (Figs. 82–83).

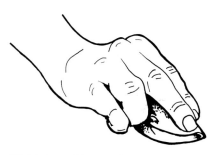

Fig 82 Hold the rubber with the thumb, small finger and third finger at the rear

Fig 83 When holding the rubber the third and small fingers are tucked up and help keep the 'tail' in place

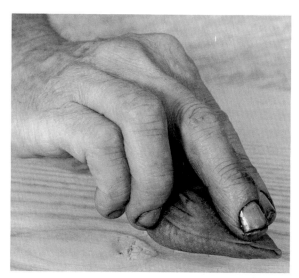

Fig 81 Hold a rubber with the index and second finger at the front – do not apply pressure with the thumb

Fig 84 Place the index and second finger over the point

When to use a rubber

After sealing   Use it to apply a thin film of polish ready for colouring. Generally use a newly made rubber with an open cloth, often called a fad.

To apply colour   Keep a rubber solely for this purpose or use an old rubber that can be thrown away after use.

After second coating   For bodying up and finishing off. Use an older rubber with a more closely woven cloth so that the polish cannot come through too quickly.

How to use a rubber – when rubbering straight

Hold the rubber as described above and ensure you apply an even pressure. The amount of pressure you require at any stage will vary but you will learn as you go along. Always rubber in the direction of the grain and as parallel to it as possible.

Fig 85   The rubber should be flexible so that it will easily get into turnings

When rubbering a tabletop, stand so that the grain runs left to right across your body. Start by rubbering the edge all the way round and then begin to rubber the face. Rubber so that the first stroke is near your body and the last stroke is not. Your rubber should come on at an edge (whether it is left or right does not matter) and with one continuous and even stroke rubber the whole width or length, depending on the direction of the grain. Your next stroke should come on at the other edge and it should overlap the previous stroke by about half. Carry on in this way until all the top is covered.

When rubbering a piece of furniture with turnings move your index finger to the front of the rubber to guide it into difficult areas (Fig. 85). Keep the pressure even and do not get too much polish into the turnings or it will look sticky.

How to charge a rubber

Once you have made a rubber you do not normally take it to pieces unless the cloth develops a hole. Never charge the rubber by opening it up and pouring polish into the wadding, as you will be disturbing the shape of the rubber each time. It also makes charging a rubber time-consuming. Opening a rubber up to charge it is an old fashioned idea, and it was done that way because at one time polish was manufactured by each individual polisher in his workshop so it would have ended up with a number of impurities in it. By pouring the polish directly into the wadding the cloth could act to sieve out the impurities. Nowadays we buy our polish ready-made to a set standard that is always free of impurities, therefore there is no need to charge the rubber up in this way.

To charge a rubber dip it into the polish so that all the wadding is thoroughly soaked

Fig 86 Charge the rubber by dipping it into the container of polish. **Do not remove the cloth**

Fig 87 Squeeze the rubber out from the neck to the tip. Do not mishape the rubber

(Fig. 86). The excess polish then needs squeezing out and this is done by squeezing with your thumb and first two fingers. Do not squeeze the sides of the rubber as this will distort the shape; instead squeeze holding the face and back of the rubber. Start by squeezing from the neck to the tip of the rubber (rather like milking a cow) (Fig. 87).

You should only use one hand to squeeze the rubber out and it should be the hand you are rubbering with. This avoids getting both hands sticky.

Never wipe the rubber on the side of the container you are working from as you will pick up dirt or hardened polish on the face of your rubber and it may then be transferred to the workpiece.

How to store a rubber

Rubbers should be kept in glass jars with airtight lids, and choose jars with a wide neck so it is easy to take them out. They will remain soft for several months in a good jar. If they go hard, throw them away: it is not worth trying to soften them up.

Squeeze out excess polish before storing, otherwise black dots will appear on the cloth; this is not detrimental in any way but looks unsightly.

13

C OLOURING

After your job has had a few initial rubbers of polish you have enough build on to allow you to see if any colouring is required. (This stage can be referred to as *colouring* or *colour matching*.) This is the section that is least understood by both lay people and even many involved in the furniture trade. You need an eye for colour, and restraint, as it is all to easy to overdo colouring and end up with a dark mess.

When a job is well colour-matched it does not look as if the colouring sequence has been carried out, but rather as if the cabinet maker has very carefully selected his timbers and thus made a very good job of the work. This is your objective.

Start the colouring process by loosely assembling the piece of furniture, i.e. putting the drawers and rest doors in place. Then place the item in the position in which it will be seen, e.g. a corner cupboard at eye level and a chair on its feet on the floor. **Always** colour a piece of furniture **in the position in which it will be seen. Never** try to colour on a work bench things that should stand on the floor.

With a set of chairs, line them up and start by colour matching all the backs together as this allows you to adjust to the colours. Next colour alternate sides and do the fronts, the most important parts, last.

You will need to stand about 2.5m (8ft) away to assess the areas that need colouring. Do not make the mistake of trying to stand on your head when looking at what needs to be coloured i.e. do not lie on the floor and look up at the top of a chair as it is unlikely to be the normal position you see it from. Every time you colour a section turn your back on it, walk away and then look back. If more colouring is not obviously needed do not do it.

When teaching, we find that one of the biggest problems at the colouring stage is that students are reluctant to stop but carry on and overdo the colouring. The work, when well done, should really look as if it is natural, well-selected timber.

Materials used for colouring

The colour chart below shows the general colours used for various woods but this can **only** be a general guide as each piece of wood from the same species of tree can vary dramatically. Always test colour; remember to keep the colour as clear as possible. Note that too strong a colour will obscure the grain.

Spirit colours

These come in a wide range of colours but we only need to use the three listed above. They are transparent so they darken without obscuring the grain. They are bought as powders and must be mixed with methylated spirits before use. We would normally mix them in glass or stout plastic containers of about 300ml so they are always ready for use.

Red and black are the spirit colours most commonly used, as a combination of the two will make a shade of brown. The more red that is added the warmer it will be and the more black, the colder it will be. Red can be used on its own (i.e. mixed with the 50:50 polish and methylated spirit) to make a piece of wood seem warmer and to 'kill' green in the wood. Green is rarely

---

Liquid colours

Transparent spirit black
spirit bismark brown (red)
spirit green

These are pre-mixed with methylated spirits in bottles and well shaken.

Dry colours (or pigments): Mainly used on:

Opaque

brown umber --------------------	dark oak
burnt sienna ----------------------	mahogany
raw umber (raw turkey) -------	walnut and teak
raw sienna ----------------------	lighter oak and teak

Keep these in small containers.

Bright orange chrome
yellow chrome
titanium white

Use these to lighten darker marks, as they are inclined to shade on some woods.

Fig 88　Side view of walnut chest ready for colouring

Mixing colours

Colours are mixed in about equal measures of polish and methylated spirit; this is because the thinned polish is easier to apply. The mixture holds the colour, the methylated spirit then evaporates and leaves the colour fixed in the polish.

When mixing colour always mix enough for the job you are doing as it will be difficult to get the same shade again. Mix in a small straight-sided container that will be easy to coat from. If you are only colouring one small area it is often best to mix the colour on the back of an old piece of garnet paper.

Different pieces of timber on one job can shade, and cross rails will usually be lighter than uprights. It is, therefore, important that you place the item in the correct position for colouring, because if you were to turn it through 180° the uprights would become the cross rails and so look lighter. Always start by colouring small defects, e.g. pin holes, first, and then colour the larger areas (Figs. 88–89).

used except to 'kill' red in a piece of timber, most often in walnut when a piece is too warm.

Dry colours/pigments

These again come in a wide range of colours but we generally stick to those listed above. They are powders so they produce solid colours and will, therefore, obliterate the grain if mixed too strongly. Care must be taken when using them. They can all be used on their own or in conjunction with the spirit colours, though you should not need to use the bright colours with the spirit colours.

How to apply colour

We generally apply colour with a swan's quill and number 6 and number 8 Zorino mops (Fig. 90). For larger areas, e.g. large table tops, we would colour with a rubber specially kept for this purpose, or an old rubber that can be thrown away afterwards.

It is usually best to colour large areas with a rubber as you will be applying the colour more thinly and, therefore, more evenly so there is less chance of getting a streaky finish. It is difficult to colour coat large areas evenly with a brush.

It is also important to follow the actual direction of the grain when colouring even if the grain is wild. This is because the

Fig 89 Coat colour evenly in strips across the full width

Fig 90 Side view of chest of drawers finished and fitted up

colouring will look artificial if it is seen to go across the grain.

When you have completed all necessary colouring, the whole job (not just those areas you have coloured) should be **second coated** or **colour fastened**, i.e. you should apply a brush coat of polish. The choice of polish will depend on the item being polished.

Colouring inside a corner cupboard

It was traditional on pine-backed corner cupboards to paint the inside green. If the inside is in a bad way it can be 'repainted' using coloured polish. The old paint first needs a good papering down with a new piece of 120 grade garnet paper, and it is best to wear a dust mask because the dust is very fine and unpleasant. Next remove the dust with a dust brush or piece of towelling.

Mix the 'paint' by using 4lb button polish thinned with equal measures of methylated spirit, then add spirit green, some raw sienna and a small amount of brown umber to obtain a solid colour. Apply two coats of the colour, papering down between coats with a pad. The result will be a dullish solid green colour, similar to the original.

Colouring leather

Leather insets, e.g. in desks and writing slopes, can be coloured and polished if they are slightly damaged. You first need to give the leather a couple of rubbers of thin button polish. You will then be able to assess the colour required. Do not try to colour too large an area at a time. A quill is usually the best brush to use.

Take some 4lb button polish thinned with equal measures of methylated spirit and add the appropriate spirit and/or pigments. After colouring, apply a few more rubbers of thin button polish. Do not apply too much polish, and never second coat leathers, because they will look unsightly.

14

SECOND COATING, BODYING UP AND FINISHING OFF

Second coating

This stage comes after colouring and involves applying a coat of polish with a brush. It serves two purposes:

To fix the colour   If you were to rubber polish over colour it could soften it and so remove some of the colour, because colour is basically very thin polish. Apply a brush coat quickly and evenly so it does not move the colour.

To provide a good foundation   When the second coating is hard it gives a good foundation of polish which can be papered very flat, so that bodying up and finishing off can take place.

Second coating should be carried out after the colour has had about ten minutes to dry. Different polishes can be used at this stage for different reasons (see Chapter 5).

If bodying up and finishing off is not required you can apply a few rubbers to the piece of furniture after papering down the second coat. The rubber should only contain a small amount of polish. The oak table in Fig. 91 was done in this way.

Fig 91   A solid oak drop leaf dining table. Finished with a few stiff rubbers. Note the clarity of the grain and evenness of the colour

Bodying up

The aim of bodying up is to fill the grain and create a full body with a good shine. This is achieved by keeping the polish pliable and pushing it into the grain. This is the part of French polishing that most people regard as the real art. It is a difficult subject to teach as so much depends on the right pressure at the right time. The approach to bodying up is straightforward but it must be practised to achieve good results every time.

It is at this stage that the work is papered flat and smooth in preparation for the application of more polish. To do this use grade 150 garnet finishing paper, and hold the paper firmly in the hand, keeping the hand as flat as possible. The paper should be lubricated with a small amount of raw linseed oil. Smear the oil lightly over the surface of the paper to be used and take care with the amount of oil used. As an alternative to oiled paper you could use a sanding pad which requires no oil.

Fig 92   When bodying up or finishing off sit comfortably and have polish, raw linseed oil and rubber jar within easy reach

If the work to be papered is open-grained use only a very small amount of oil, in order to stop it soaking into the grain. On close-grained timbers, such as mahogany or walnut, you can use slightly more oil. When papering with the lubricated paper use a circular action with care to create a very flat surface. You can also use sanding pads in this manner.

When papering moulds and edges, take extra care, and shape the paper to the mould with the hand, avoiding papering through the polish and colour on edges. Do not use cork blocks to get a flat surface at this stage as the flat block will not follow slight undulations in the same way as the hand.

Now remove all dust and finger marks with a clean duster. The position in which you body up needs to be comfortable and well-lit, because you need to observe the surface closely at all times (Fig. 92). Have within easy reach your container of polish, small pot of raw linseed oil, bottle of methylated spirit and your rubber jar.

Take your rubber, ensuring that it is of good shape and flexible, immerse it into the thin polish you have selected and carefully squeeze out into the polish container about 50 per cent of the polish in the rubber. Now wipe over the surface evenly in straight lines about four times, taking care not to get any wet patches of polish. Do not allow the rubber to stop while in contact with the surface. Hold the rubber gently but firmly using little pressure with the thumb. Pressure used in polishing is gradually built up as the rubber dries.

You will now observe a flat surface, damp with polish and slight amounts of open grain. To fill this grain and keep the surface flat, now use a circular action. To lubricate the rubber and so stop it from sticking, put a small amount of oil on the

Fig 93 When using oil to lubricate during bodying up or finishing off it should be applied to the base of the rubber. Dip the thumb into the pot of oil

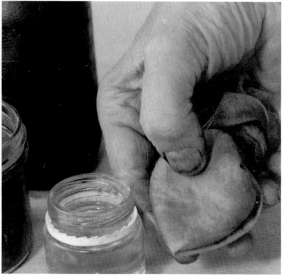

Fig 94 Put a small amount of oil onto the bottom of the rubber and then spread it evenly over the polished surface

end of your thumb and transfer it to the rubber surface (Fig. 93–94). The oil is then spread with straight lines over the whole surface.

Now begin the circular actions, using an even system of covering the surface. We usually divide, for example, a top or side into four or five lines of circles in the direction of the grain. Each line should overlap the other and the edges. The moulds are rubbered evenly from time to time to ensure there is as much polish on them as on the top.

When we are carrying out the sequence on a top we never start in the same spot on the work when we have recharged the rubber – we find it best to start in different corners spreading the new polish and oil over the surface (Fig. 95). A gradual build up of polish is achieved, and the rubber needs to be dipped into the polish as it dries out and more oil is applied. Too much oil must not be used and occasionally

Fig 95 Always come on at a corner, and alternate the corners so you do not get a build up of polish at any one corner

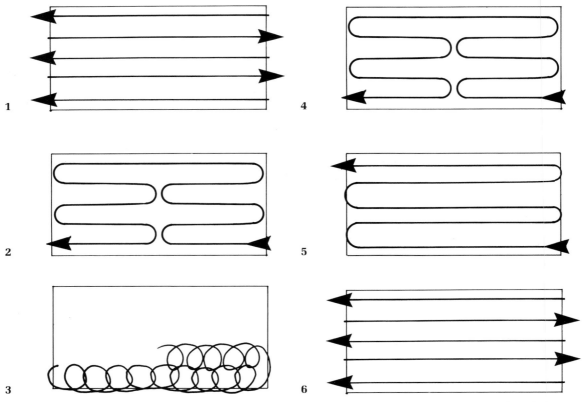

Fig 96 Sequence of rubber movements when bodying up or finishing off:

1 Apply a few straight rubbers of polish
2 Apply oil to the rubber and spread it over the work
3 Start circular movements. Cover the area with four or five rows of circles, each row overlapping. Ensure you go over the edges
4 When starting to remove the oil go from circular movements to elongated strokes (or figures-of-eight if you can manage then; we prefer the elongated movement as it is easier to maintain)
5 Lengthen the movements but do not come off at the edges
6 Straighten out the strokes, coming off at each edge. The last few strokes with methylated spirit in the rubber should be light and come off at each edge

more polish (only) can be taken into the rubber, using existing oil on the surface.

The amount of polish applied at this stage is purely a matter of personal taste. We prefer to start removing the oil as soon as the grain is filled. This leaves a full, thin polish which, on some occasions, is suitable for a finish. When removing the oil we will still use a circular action with just the thin polish in the rubber and a reasonable amount of pressure. This has the effect of keeping the oil on top of the polished surface. When the oil starts to disappear we revert to straight lines and using less pressure. Subsequent applications of polish are well squeezed out and a small amount of methylated spirit is applied to the rubber.

The straight line action is now always started at the edge nearest to you and the action takes the rubber off the work at each stroke. Every line with the rubber should slightly overlap the previous one, ensuring that the surface is fully covered. With practice, try to use as little methylated spirits as possible, as too much can soften the surface, spoiling it.

The problems that may occur at this time are having the rubber too wet or applying too much pressure with the rubber, leaving whip marks (marks of polish generally across the grain). If the rubber is too wet the surface will quickly become sticky and the rubber will not move smoothly across the surface. Whip marks are the result of pressure in relation to the dampness of the rubber; pressure must not be used in circular action until the rubber is drying out. In both cases the best remedy is to put the work to one side for half an hour. Then take an old piece of fine garnet paper with oil on it and flatten out the offending fault before carrying on.

Finishing off

This process in many ways is a repeat of bodying up, and you will see that after leaving overnight the bodied up surface will have settled slightly. If all the oil has been removed and there are no faults with the surface the work could be considered finished.

If more polish is required for a higher build, repeat the bodying up process, though this time very little papering should be needed. We would normally use an old piece of oiled 150 or 180 grade garnet paper just to abrade the surface. You will find that the bodying up process is this time much quicker, as less polish needs to be applied and, therefore, the rubber is used drier. Take care when finishing to remove all traces of oil from the surface (Fig. 96).

Fig 97 An indifferent display cabinet can be made to look desirable after a full polish

Spiriting off

This process follows finishing off and is designed to give an extra high shine, particularly on pianos. It is, however, very rarely practised today as it requires an expert hand and great care.

To spirit off, the grain needs to be thoroughly choked. The polish is gently papered with an old piece of oiled paper. A new rubber is made which is charged only with methylated spirit. A little oil is applied to the rubber and is then spread over the surface. Circular movements are carried out as previously until the oil has almost gone, then it is straightened out.

Fig 98   Chairs can be rather awkward but a severely damaged balloon back can be given a new lease of life

Tearing

Practice the spiriting off process at your peril as it will be all too easy to over soften the surface and 'tear' it. Tearing is where the rubber is too wet in relation to the amount of pressure used. It shows as a dull streak with the polished surface broken or torn. This normally happens at the final finishing stage and generally occurs when applying the final few rubbers. No pressure should be used whatsoever, particularly if giving a rubber of methylated spirit. It just needs the rubber to glide on the surface but it is most important that the whole surface is covered evenly.

It is a mistaken idea that the French polisher uses a great amount of pressure all the time. The pressure is used mainly to flatten the body of polish at the bodying up and finishing stages, when the rubber is lubricated with raw linseed oil and is really quite dry, and the object is to have the grain filled and the surface very flat.

If at any stage of polishing you encounter the problems of tearing or whips put the job to one side overnight. The next day paper it flat with an old piece of oiled paper and start again from where you left off (Figs. 97–98).

15

CLEANING DOWN AND REPOLISHING WITHOUT STRIPPING

Sometimes a piece of furniture is not bad enough to strip down but is only dirty. You can clean down a piece and then polish over it to make it look bright and fresh.

Cleaning down a polished surface

There are several methods of cleaning down and the list below starts with the mildest and ends with the most severe. If you are unsure of how much cleaning is required start at the top of the list and if that is not strong enough work your way down until it is clean enough:

- Briwax
- raw linseed oil and pure turpentine in equal measures
- raw linseed oil, pure turpentine and methylated spirit in equal measures
- raw linseed oil, pure turpentine, methylated spirit and vinegar in equal measures
- raw linseed oil, pure turpentine, methylated spirit, vinegar and warm water in equal measures
- washing soda in hot water
- 0.880 ammonia in hot water

Fig 99   Briwax is a good general cleaner as it is a
mild abrasive wax. When using Briwax only
tackle small areas as it is a hard wax that is
difficult to spread. It is ideal for use on items
that are dirty but where the polish is still in
a good condition and does not require
stripping

Briwax

A very good cleaner where the surface is
basically smooth but dirty. You will not
need to French polish afterwards (Fig. 99).
Start by applying some wax to a small area
and, rubbing vigorously, you should see
the dirt come off. Because it is an abrasive
wax it will clean and polish at the same
time. Briwax should not be used as a
general household wax as it is too hard.

Note: After using the following cleaners
in the appropriate manner you need to
paper the piece of furniture smooth and
then apply French polish.

Raw linseed oil and pure turpentine

Mixed in equal measures, this is a good
general cleaner, and should be applied

with a piece of towelling and rubbed
vigorously. If dirt is a little stubborn use a
piece of 0000 steel wool gently in the
direction of the grain. This can be pre-
mixed and kept in a glass jar ready for use.

Raw linseed oil, pure turpentine and methylated spirit

Mixed in equal measures, this can be used
in the same manner as the above cleaner.
This can also be pre-mixed ready for use
(Fig. 100). Shake well before use as it will
settle into two layers.

Raw linseed oil, pure turpentine, methylated spirit and vinegar

Mixed in equal measures, this can be used
in the same manner as the above cleaner.
Because of the presence of the vinegar
(malt will suffice) this cleaner is more
aggressive in its properties so take care
that you do not overdo the cleaning and
risk attacking the polish. Mix just enough
to do the job as it will not store well, and
keep well-shaken as it will settle into
layers.

Raw linseed oil, pure turpentine, methylated spirit, vinegar and warm water

Mixed in equal measures. Use in the same
manner as above cleaner. Use only freshly
mixed as the water should be warm during
use. Do not store but keep well-shaken
during use as it will settle out.

Washing soda crystals dissolved in hot water

Use rubber gloves and apply with a piece
of towelling and rub vigorously. Grade
0000 steel wool can be used if dirt is

stubborn. It is only really effective whilst hot so always mix fresh. It is best not to use this on veneered jobs in case it softens underlying glue.

0.880 ammonia (e.g. Jeyes cloudy ammonia)

A very good, strong cleaner. Wear rubber gloves and do not mix too strong as the fumes are powerful; about half an egg-cupful to 2.5l (½ gal.) will suffice. Use in a well-ventilated room. Apply liberally with a piece of towelling and rub vigorously. You can use grade 0000 steel wool, rubbing in the direction of the grain, but take care. This is a powerful cleaner so make sure the polish is not starting to perish or it may remove both dirt and polish.

For very dirty jobs you can use scouring powder in conjunction with ammonia water – apply to the wet cloth and rub vigorously. We have used this method on old church pews that have been heavily varnished and engrained with dirt from frequent use. After using ammonia water or soda water wash down with clean water.

Preparing and repolishing

If there are any holes they should be filled. Because there is polish on the surface you should not fill with Brummer or epoxy filler because you would need to sand them down and you could sand through the polish, creating more problems for yourself. We would fill holes at this stage with a coloured hard beeswax.

How to make a coloured beeswax

Melt a small quantity of hard (block) beeswax in a tin can standing in a pan of hot water, adding suitable colour pig-

Fig 100   Raw linseed oil, pure turpentine and methylated spirit in equal measures is a mild cleaner which is ideal for use on an item that is very dirty. Keep the mixture well-shaken as it will settle out. Do not clean too large an area at a time. If the job is particularly dirty a piece of grade 0000 steel wool can be used after the mixture has been applied

Pigments used for making coloured beeswax	
For light shades, e.g. teak, light oak	raw sienna
Cold, medium shades, e.g. walnut	raw umber
Warm medium shades, e.g. mid oak	brown umber
Dark oak	raw umber and brown umber
Mahogany and rosewood	brown umber and burnt sienna

Fig 101   When filling a hole on a piece of furniture that has polish on it a coloured beeswax should be used. Wax can be made or bought in a range of colours

ments (e.g. brown umber to make a coloured wax suitable for dark oak) and stir well. Pour the coloured wax into a mould to harden. If you do not have a mould pour the wax into a container of cold water and quickly squeeze the wax into a ball whilst it is still in the water.

Filling holes

To fill holes with beeswax you need a blunt penknife (a smoker's one is best). Push the wax into the hole with the penknife and remove the surplus with the back of the knife (Figs. 101–102). You can paper it later to make sure the area is flat.

Once all holes have been filled you need to paper the surface to ensure it is flat and smooth. Use an old piece of grade 120 or 150 garnet paper or one of the sanding pads.

Repolishing

It is always best to use 4lb button polish on top of old polish as it will dry readily and is less liable to react adversely with underlying polish. Apply two or three straight rubbers so that it acquires a sheen and you can see what needs to be coloured.

Colouring

Colour as in Chapter 13 and fix any colouring with a thin coat of button polish. If no colouring is required do not second coat as you do not want to put more polish on than is necessary. Paper flat with a pad

Fig 102   Using the back of the knife excess wax
should be removed to leave the surface
flat. It can now be polished over if necessary

or an old piece of garnet paper if you have
second coated.

Finishing

It is best to finish with just a few straight
rubbers as there is already plenty of polish.
It is possible to body up and/or finish off
but we would not normally recommend it
as there could be poor adhesion with the
old polish, so the less new polish that is
put on the better. For bodying up and
finishing off see Chapter 14.

Polishing unseen areas

We would not generally strip and repolish
the backs of table leaves, inside cupboards,
the backs of cupboard doors or inside chair
frames. The aim is that they should look
clean, and in order to do this we would
clean them down with ammonia water.
Paper the surface smooth with 100 grade
garnet paper and then apply a brush coat
of button polish.

Colour may be added to the polish if a
darker colour is required (see Chapter 13),
and for this we would usually use up any
spare colour we have left from another
job.

16

POLISHING INLAID WORK

The method of polishing inlaid work does not significantly differ from the sequence involved in polishing solid timber or veneered timber with no inlay. The main problems arise in the use of stains, as oil stains for example will stain the main timber and the inlay if the right procedure is not taken.

The stages to follow when restoring inlaid work are:

Stage 1

Follow procedures for stripping as in Chapter 6. Some earlier books on French polishing suggest that you never strip veneered or inlaid furniture as it will soften the underlying glue and so raise the veneers. This is nonsense: the only care that needs to be taken is that you thoroughly wet the surface with stripper so that when you scrape it off it comes off easily without you having to dig in the scraper, so avoiding damage. When neutralizing it is best not to use ammonia water as it may over wet the veneers. Instead use methylated spirit or turpentine substitute.

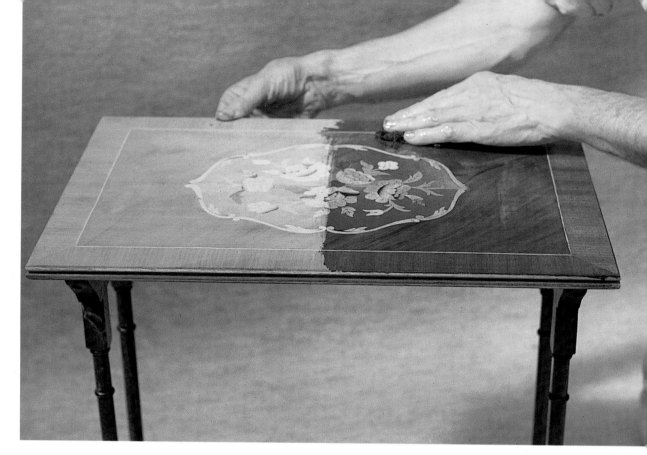

Fig 103 Using raw linseed oil and pure turpentine as a stain on a reproduction inlaid table

Stage 2

Make any necessary repairs and fill all holes with epoxy or Brummer filler. When papering start with grade 80 garnet paper in order to get out deep marks and then work through the grades to finish with grade 150 garnet paper. Ensure that you have removed all papering marks.

Stage 3

Decide on the colour you require and choose one of the three following types of stains:

- raw linseed oil and pure turpentine
- bichromate of potash
- oil stain

Raw linseed oil and pure turpentine

Mix equal measures of raw linseed oil and pure turpentine and apply with a piece of towelling to the prepared surface quite liberally. Wipe off the excess with a clean piece of towelling in the direction of the grain.

This stain should be left to dry for at least 24 hours, after which time it will be as dark as it can possibly go. It may have darkened a little from when it was first applied.

This is a chemical stain and will act only on certain timbers, mainly mahogany, walnut, rosewood and very old oak. It will darken only the main timber and will not affect the inlay or stringing. The colour achieved will depend on the natural colour of the timber and it will serve to greatly enhance the beauty and clarity of the wood.

This is the stain we use most frequently on inlaid and older furniture. Try it for yourself – we are sure you will be delighted with the results (Fig. 103). You will also love the smell. However, do note that raw linseed oil and pure turpentine will not really have much effect on new timber.

Bichromate of potash

This is another chemical stain but it needs to be mixed in warm water first. Bichromate is bought as fine crystals and is best stored as such, so do not mix up litres (gallons) in advance as it will not keep for very long in its mixed state.

If a strong solution is mixed the final colour will be darker so you will need to experiment with mixing in order to achieve the required shade. Always mix sufficient to stain the job in hand as it will be very difficult to mix another batch of stain to the same colour. The colour cannot be judged until polish has been applied.

It is best when used on mahogany, whether it is inlaid or not. If used on inlaid woods it will not affect the inlays. If bichromate is used on new wood this needs to be dampened with clean water first then left overnight to dry. The workpiece is then papered down gently after which the timber is ready to be stained.

Apply the stain with a piece of towelling and wear rubber gloves. Take care when applying bichromate as it bites into the timber quickly and can leave marks where unevenly applied. Apply it as wet as possible and wipe off the excess with a clean piece of towelling in the direction of the grain. It then needs 24 hours to dry. Then paper the workpiece to flatten the raised grain.

Oil stains

If the two stains above do not give you the colour you require you should consider using oil stains. You can use them on inlaid work but take care to avoid staining the inlay.

The inlay needs to be 'painted out', i.e. heat resisting pale polish is coated on to all areas of inlay as this will stop the stain biting into these areas. It can be a laborious job, and requires a steady hand. A swan's quill is usually the best brush for coating inlay (Figs. 104–5).

Allow the polish to dry for a few minutes and then apply the oil stain with a piece of towelling. Apply liberally and wipe off the excess with a clean piece of towelling. Leave to dry for at least 4 hours.

Because the inlay has to be coated in this way it must also be scraped off at a later date so that the inlay can look clean. Do this after colouring, but before second coating, and use a penknife. Take care that you do not scrape off any polish or colour around it.

Stage 4

After staining the whole job needs a coat of heavy white sealer. When this is dry the workpiece needs papering smooth with either an old pad or an old piece of grade 150 garnet paper.

Stage 5

If the inlay work needs to be kept as light as possible, use heat resisting pale polish from now on, but if it does not matter, use 4lb button polish. Give the job three or four straight rubbers. You should now have a smooth, clean surface with a sheen that will allow you to see any areas that need colouring (Fig. 106).

Fig 104 'Painting out' inlay with polish to stop oil stain biting

Stage 6

If you need to colour the main timber and not the inlay mix the right colours (see Chapter 13) and apply by either rubber or Zorino mop. If you need to coat colour over the inlay do so, as this can be scraped clean later.

    After colouring is complete scrape the inlay/stringing clean, to remove the polish

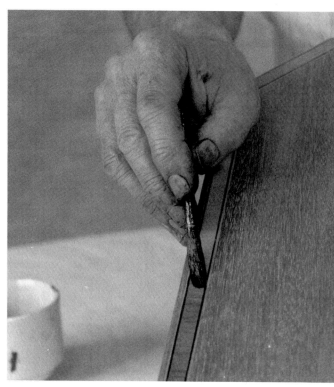

Fig 105 Coat inlay with heat resisting pale polish if you wish to stain with oil stain as it will stop the stain striking in the area of the polish

Fig 106 One chair after staining – note that the inlay is still clean

you coated on before staining and colouring (Fig. 107). The inlay/stringing will then look clean and sharp (Figs 108). If you need to colour the stringing do so at this stage.

If boxwood stringing is to be coloured, the colours you are likely to need are titanium white, yellow chrome and orange chrome. Mix a little polish and methylated spirit together and add a combination of the above colours to it. You will need to experiment quite a bit before you get it right. If you apply colour and think that it is very wrong wipe it off with a damp

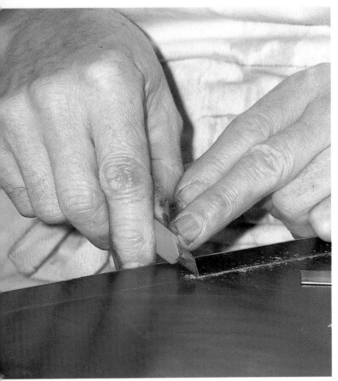

Fig 107 Scraping inlay clean with a knife before second coating

rubber and try again. You can mix a small amount of colour on the back of a piece of old garnet paper.

Stage 7

Second coat with the relevant polish (see Chapter 5) and allow to dry. When dry, cut back with an old piece of grade 150 garnet paper (with a little linseed oil applied to the surface to lubricate the paper and stop it scratching the polish), at the same time flattening it.

Stage 8

Body up and finish off as in Chapter 14.

Fig 108 Stringing on a table base after it has been scraped and second coated

17

E BONIZING

Any wood can in theory be ebonized but it is best if only close-grained wood is used, e.g. mahogany and beech. Victorian ebonized furniture would more often than not have been mahogany. Modern ebonized furniture will most likely be beech. The method of ebonizing is the same for both mahogany and beech, or whether you are ebonizing a new piece or re-ebonizing an old one.

Ebonized furniture should be a solid black colour with no grain showing and the grain pores should be filled. The surface should also be flat and free from defects and it should be glossy. Excellent timber preparation is essential as a black, glossy finish will show up every defect. Ebonized furniture is most likely to have been stained with black water stain as it penetrates into the timber.

Stage 1

If you are re-ebonizing a piece of furniture strip in the normal way (see Chapter 6). Fill holes and sand to remove any faults. You do not have to paper all the old stain out as this will in fact help to darken the job. If you are ebonizing a new piece or a

Fig 109   A beech chair being stained with black oil stain before ebonizing

sealer. When dry, paper it smooth (Fig. 110).

stripped piece not previously ebonized ensure that you have removed all faults.

Stage 2

Stain with either black oil stain or black water stain as you prefer (Fig. 109). Remember with a water stain that it will raise the grain of new timber so you must pre wet it. You can add pigments to the oil stain to make a more solid colour, e.g. lamp black. Whatever stain you use the objective is to get the bare wood as black as possible.

Stage 3

You should then seal it with heavy white

Stage 4

Add some spirit black to the button polish you will be using and apply three or four rubbers of this polish. You will now be able to see if areas need colouring.

Stage 5

It is unlikely that you will need to do any colouring, unless there is an area you have filled that has not taken stain. In this case the only colour you will need is black (spirit black and/or lamp black).

Stage 6

If you have coloured you should now second coat with the same tinted polish

Fig 110 The beech chair stained black and ready to polish

Fig 111 An attractive, rush-seated, child's chair of beech, which has been ebonized

you have already been using. Paper the second coat carefully then carry on polishing with the black polish until you have built up enough shine.

Stage 7

For the best effect the final rubbers should be with button polish tinted with spirit red as this, for some reason, makes the black look clearer (Fig. 111).

18

*D*ULLING AND WAXING

Dulling

The process of bodying up will result in a high shine which not all people find attractive. If you wish to reduce the shine on a surface it needs to be dulled. Dulling involves gently abrading the surface so that a large number of very fine scratches are put in the surface. This means that light is refracted and will not, therefore, reflect in the same manner. If you wish to dull down a polished surface there are several techniques:

- using a dulling brush
- using pumice powder and a dulling brush
- using wax and grade 0000 steel wool

Using a dulling brush

A dulling brush is like a large shoe brush – it should be of good quality and reasonably stiff. In order to dull in this manner the brush needs to be gently passed over the surface in even strokes in the direction of the grain. Always ensure that you brush evenly along the entire length of a piece to be dulled. Do not apply pressure when brushing but keep the movement light and

Fig 112 Apply pumice powder to the job using the pumice bag

Fig 113 Gently and evenly brush the pumice with a dulling brush to abrade the surface and so dull it

flowing. This is the gentlest form of dulling, as the bristles are acting as the abrading agents.

Using a dulling brush and pumice

You need to make a pumice bag in order to follow this technique. For the older readers among you it is like a dolly bag that is filled with pumice. For those younger readers take a 150mm (6in) square of a closely woven cloth and place a small amount of pumice in the centre, draw up the corners and tie up with string close to the ball of pumice. This should be kept in the container of pumice and placed on the top so that it is ready for use.

When using pumice for dulling apply it to the job and not to the brush. Use the pumice bag by bouncing it onto the job so that a light but even coat of pumice is applied (Figs. 112–113). Then use the pumice brush in light, even strokes along

the whole length of the job in the direction of the grain. Be careful not to apply too much pressure as this method of dulling is quite severe.

Never brush round in circles as if scrubbing or you will score the surface rather than dull it. Dust off any excess powder with a soft cloth in the direction of the grain.

Using wax and grade 0000 steel wool

This is probably the best method of dulling for those people who are a little hesitant about the process. First apply a soft wax to the job with a piece of towelling and ensure that it is spread evenly all over (Figs. 114–115). Then take a decent-sized piece of grade 0000 steel wool and rub gently in the direction of the grain along the entire length of the job, keeping the pressure even. Do not rub round in circles with the steel wool.

Fig 114 Apply wax with a piece of towelling. A darker wax is used here for emphasis, though we normally select a colour of wax closest to the colour of the wood

Fig 115 With a piece of grade 0000 steel wool rub gently in the direction of the grain to dull the surface

Waxing for maintenance

The aim of waxing is to nourish the timber and stop it from drying out, especially now that so many people live in centrally-heated houses. Waxing should not be done too often or it will build up and make the surface too sticky. You do not need to wax something that you have recently polished, but should aim to wax about twice a year.

Use a pure beeswax polish and not one with carnauba wax in, as it will be too hard to spread. Though there are many available off the shelf, you can easily make your own wax polish.

Making wax polish

The most basic method is to take a solid block of beeswax (bleached or natural) and melt it in a tin standing in boiling water, then add pure turpentine. As the turpen-tine is highly flammable, avoid heating the mixture over a naked flame (i.e. electric ring rather than gas cooker). The amount of turpentine you need to add will depend on how soft a wax polish you want, so experiment. The ideal consistency should be like that of butter at room temperature. If you wish to make a coloured wax polish add some pigment to the melted wax and stir well. To make an antique wax suitable for dark oak and mahogany mix in brown umber, again experiment to get the colour you want.

This recipe appears in *The Care of Antiques* by John Fitzmaurice Mills (Arlington, 1980):

85g (3oz)	Purified beeswax
230g (8fl oz)	Pure turpentine
230g (8fl oz)	Water
a few drops	Ammonia

Break up the wax into small pieces and melt, remove from heat, add turps and then water stirring rapidly to achieve an even mix. Finally add a few drops of ammonia to thicken the mixture to a cream.

Wax polish is best kept in a tin with a tight lid. It should be applied thinly and buffed up to give a sheen but with no obvious build up of wax. Over many years these thin applications will build up but you will not notice it as it is a gradual process.

When using wax most people will get a clean cloth and take some wax from the top of the container and try and spread it over the job. However, in this way they usually end up with a large amount of wax polish in the area where it was initially placed and very little elsewhere. Buffing it up then becomes difficult as there is a concentration of fairly firm wax in one area, and this will eventually build up and become sticky so unsightly finger marks are left.

To avoid putting too much wax on, slightly dampen a piece of towelling with pure turpentine and place on the top of the wax in the tin. When you need to wax a job you can take out the cloth wiping a little wax from the top and spread it evenly over the job. When you come to buffing up it will be easy as there is only a small amount of wax on the surface. Keep the cloth in the tin so that it is always ready for use.

Types of wax

A wide range of waxes is available and the main ones we use are:

- normal white polishing wax
- matt white wax
- antique polishing wax
- teak wax
- clear Briwax

White polishing wax   This is a thin beeswax and is used as a protective surface only after French polishing has finished. It should not be used too soon after polishing, so leave at least a week before waxing the polished surface.

Matt wax   A very thin beeswax which dries to a matt finish. It is used when a piece of furniture does not require a high gloss.

Antique polishing wax   This wax is used on dark furniture, particularly oak, when there are carvings. The wax is thin and easily rubs onto turnings and carvings. When rubbed into carvings with a clean piece of towelling and brushed with a good shoe brush, this gives a very good clean finish.

Teak wax   This is a wax specially blended for teak furniture. It is quite a greasy wax to stop the teak drying out. It is particularly good on pine which has been coated with pre-catalyzed lacquer then waxed and flattened with fine steel wool.

Briwax   This is made from a blend of carnauba (vegetable) wax and beeswax. We only use it for cleaning antiques (see Chapter 15) where the surface is in good condition but is dirty, and only a small area, 300mm (12in) square can be done at a time.

All the waxes are applied in the same way, by having a piece of towelling permanently in the tin; it absorbs enough wax for the process. This is spread over the surface and burnished up with a clean piece of towelling.

19

COMMON PROBLEMS

Among the most common problems you will encounter either during or after French polishing are:

- chilling of the polish
- sweating of the polish
- chinese writing
- white marks
- scratches
- fading of all or part of the job

Chilling

This is where the polish looks milky white or cloudy and is caused by working in a damp and/or draughty atmosphere during any stage of polishing. You will be able to see it chill as you work.

The easiest solution is to place it near a source of heat: dry heat rather than a naked flame. When the damp bloom has dried the polishing can be continued with. To avoid this happening in the first place always work in a warm room with good ventilation but no draughts.

Sweating

This usually occurs several weeks after finishing off and shows itself as very fine

Fig 116   Mahogany cutlery table after being
exposed to damp and strong sunlight

cracks in the polished surface which
exude oil. It can be caused if raw linseed
oil and pure turpentine were used as a
stain and not allowed to dry for long
enough. However, this problem is generally caused by using too much oil at the
bodying up and/or the finishing off stage
and the failure to work it out.

To cure it, clean down the surface with
equal measures of raw linseed oil and
methylated spirit to remove any grease
and to soften the surface. Then paper it
with an old piece of grade 150 garnet paper
that has been lubricated with a touch of
raw linseed oil. Ensure that the surface is
flat and smooth.

The next stage is basically finishing off
again and you will still need to use oil to
lubricate your rubber but this time take
care to work it all out. See Chapter 14 on
how to finish off. The aim is to work the
oil out and not particularly to build up
more polish so the process should not take
too long.

Chinese writing

This shows as a series of quite obvious
cracks running in all directions (Fig. 117).
It happens for two main reasons:

Use of incompatible polishes See
Chapter 5. For example, if you had second
coated with 50:50 pale amber varnish and
button polish and then finished off with
heat resisting pale polish you would get
Chinese writing. It will usually take
several years to appear, but we have
known it to occur in a matter of only
weeks. This happens because the polishes
have different hardening properties, e.g.
when the polish used last hardens faster
than underlying polishes, it will cause the
whole surface to crack because the
pressures are unequal.

The only way to solve this problem is to
strip and repolish the whole area that is

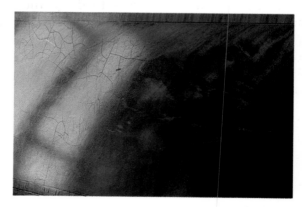

Fig 117   Part of an Edwardian wardrobe showing
how polish can crack to produce Chinese
writing. This is usually the result of using
two incompatible polishes

affected. Ensure that you use compatible polishes next time.

Very bright sunlight The heat of the sun will break down the polish over a number of years causing the polish to crack.

White marks

These can be caused when water or alcohol becomes trapped in the polish and is the result of one of three things:

Spilt water If water is left lying on the polished surface for sometime the surface will become marked. This is commonly caused when plants are over-watered and excess water is not wiped away.

Spilt alcohol This (including perfume) will mark the surface if it is not wiped off straight away.

Cups When these contain a hot drink and the base of the cup is damp, the heat from the liquid will drive the dampness on the bottom of the cup into the polish (as steam) where it will become trapped.

In order to remove these marks heat must be generated in order to drive the trapped water or alcohol out of the polish (Fig. 118). There are several methods of doing this which are listed below. The first is the mildest, the last is the most severe and the most alarming.

Raw linseed oil rub a little vigorously into the area of the mark, this may generate enough heat to remove it.

Cigar ash/raw linseed oil Rub a little vigorously in the area of the mark.

Mild abrasive (such as T-cut) This should only be used where there is no

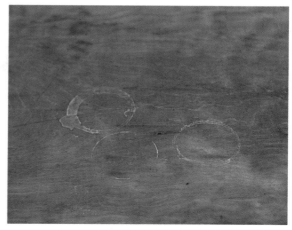

Fig 118 A white ring mark is usually caused when a cup with a damp base and containing a hot liquid is left on the surface for some time. The heat from the liquid causes the dampness on the base of the cup to be driven into the polish as steam where it becomes trapped

open grain as when the T-cut dries it leaves a white residue which will settle in the grain.

Methylated spirit/matches The quickest and, in our opinion, the most effective method. Dampen a piece of towelling with methylated spirit and have a match ready to light (a lighter is not really suitable). Then gently wipe the cloth over the mark and immediately apply the match to this area (Fig. 119). Take care that the hand with the cloth and the hand with the match do not come into contact. The amount of methylated spirit you put on is very minimal so the flame will go out in seconds and if it does not, blow it out. You will very often see the mark disappear as you watch, and if it does not you can try again after a few minutes (Fig. 120). This method does not usually harm the polish so once the mark has been removed you can wax the surface.

Fig 119 The most dramatic way to remove a white ring mark is to drive it out with heat. Slightly dampen a cloth with methylated spirit and wipe it over the area of the ring, then immediately apply a lighted match to it – this will drive the trapped moisture out. The flames should go out almost immediately because there should be very little methylated spirit on the surface. You may blow out the flame if you wish. The mark will normally be removed at the first attempt but if it has only partly gone the process can be repeated several times. Always allow several minutes between attempts so that the polish does not become soft

Scratches

If the scratches are shallow the surface can be repolished as the polish will fill in the scratches. If the scratch is deep or if it is a dent fill the hole with an appropriately coloured hard beeswax (Figs. 101–102). Colour and repolish as necessary (see Chapter 15).

If there is deep scratch across the grain, especially if it is on a tabletop, it is usually best to strip and repolish the whole top as marks across the grain when filled and coloured usually shade quite badly. However, scratches with the grain are easy to disguise.

Fading

Fading is caused by exposure to light, and though it cannot be stopped it can be minimized by ensuring that a piece of furniture is kept out of strong sunlight.

If the whole or part of a job has faded the only solution is to strip and repolish it all (Fig. 116). A common occurrence is a dining table with a spare leaf that is not used. The top that is exposed will fade and the spare leaf that is often kept inside

Fig 120   After the white mark has been removed it should be left for a short while and can then be waxed with a soft beeswax. It is not usually necessary to repolish the area

the table will not. When stripping and repolishing it is important that all the leaves are stripped including the spare one as it will be far easier to get them all the same colour again. Once the old polish is stripped off and sanded the original colour will return.

Plaster of paris filler in the grain

During the late Victorian and Edwardian periods plaster of paris was increasingly used as a grain filler, and pigments were added to it to obtain the required colour. Due to exposure to light the pigment within the filler often fades to reveal the white plaster of paris in the grain. This is particularly common in mahogany and walnut furniture (Fig. 122).

Fig 121   Detail of French desk, once filled with epoxy resin which is now ready to be coloured out

Fig 122 An attractive Edwardian inlaid table –
note that the plaster of paris grain filler is
obvious when the piece is stripped

Fig 123 Detail of a French escritoire – the veneer
has broken due to movement of the sub-
frame

If you encounter a piece of furniture
with this problem the only way to solve it
will be to strip off the old polish and paper
the filler out. The process of stripping and
neutralizing will help to remove some of
the filler but you will have to remove the
bulk of it by papering. It is an unpleasant
task as it usually requires far more papering than would normally be necessary
when preparing the timber.

The modern thixotropic grain fillers are
suitable for use if you wish to grain fill an
item again. Exposure to sunlight will
ultimately affect this type of filler but it
will fade evenly and will not leave a white
residue in the grain.

Movement of sub-frame

This is basically a cabinet making fault
(whether made in ignorance or because of
poor quality timber) when a piece of
furniture is made on a frame and veneered
over. With movement of the timber during
the drying out process the overlaying
veneers may split (Fig. 123).

One of the most common occurrences
of this fault is on Victorian chests of
drawers, where solid pine ends are glued
to drawer runners and veneered over.
During the process of drying out the pine
cannot move and, therefore, splits down
the centre in the direction of the grain. The
veneer will also break because of the
movement.

In order to rectify this problem it is
usually necessary to strip off the old polish
and then repair the damage. It may be a
case of filling the split with an epoxy filler
or with timber filling pieces. In some cases
the sub-frame may also need repairing and
veneers may need replacing. After all
repairs have been carried out the polishing
process can begin. It will be probable that
the repaired areas will need colouring at
the correct stage (Fig. 121).

Sappy edge requiring colouring

The use of timber with a sap still visible
is generally a Victorian or later occurrence
and it was generally just a matter of being
economical and cost conscious of timber.
Such sappy edges are generally only

Fig 124   Detail of Loo table base – note the sappy
edge that requires colouring

visible once the old polish has been
stripped off as the piece would have been
coloured originally to disguise these areas
(Fig. 124).

Most people would generally not wish
to see the sappy edges so they can be
coloured out at a later stage. If timber has
been particularly selected to show a sappy
edge the polishing process is simple as no
colouring is required.

To a polisher it is not a problem of any
consequence if on the edge of a piece of
furniture, as colouring is made easier. It
is more of a problem when table tops had
been glued up with the sap on the inside
joints and, therefore, the colouring has to
be done against a straight joint. Here, a
little more patience and practice is
required.

PART THREE
PROJECTS

20

WALNUT CHEST OF DRAWERS

Fig 125 Front view of antique walnut and pine chest of drawers before polishing

This chest of drawers dates from about 1730 and is the base of a chest-on-chest. It has had a top put on to convert it into a single chest, possibly in Victorian times, and the top moulds on both edges are not original. The handles are not original either but are old and in an acceptable style. The drawers did not fit well because the drawer runners were worn, so the drawers fell a little, and the back right foot was broken.

The carcase is pine, the drawer fronts are veneered in walnut and the replaced top and moulds are mahogany. The pine sides had been scumbled originally to simulate walnut. The chest had been in a damp garage for some years and was very dirty and the polish was badly perished in places (Fig. 125).

We started by removing the handles and discovered that they were of several very slightly different styles. The handles were too dirty to be left as they were so we cleaned them by placing some soda crystals in an aluminium foil dish. We placed the handles on top and then poured on boiling water. A chemical reaction then took place by which the dirt was attracted to the side of the aluminium dish. Not all the dirt was removed by this method but it made cleaning up with a proprietary cleaner far easier than it would have been. We then repaired the foot and fitted wider drawer runners so that they were no longer slack when in.

We tried to clean the drawer fronts to retain the original patina but they were too bad. Therefore we stripped the drawers and carcase with a methyl chloride stripper. When we stripped the sides the scumbling was not affected at all, presumably because it would have been of a milk paint base. There was not much polish on (it was mainly wax). This and years of accumulated dirt came off easily with steel wool.

We neutralized the whole job with ammonia water and rubbed it down with a clean piece of grade 3 steel wool to get it as clean as possible. Because the veneers are quite thick we did not need to worry about the water softening the underlying glue.

There were many small holes including worm holes that we filled with either Brummer or epoxy filler. After the filler was dry we papered everything down with grade 80 garnet paper to remove the worst marks. We did not want to remove all the marks or it would have looked wrong, for you must expect some wear after 260 years. We papered the sides carefully so as not to remove the scumble. The final grade of paper we used on the carcase was grade 120 and on the veneered drawers grade 150.

We did not want to stain the drawer fronts with the 50:50 mix of raw linseed oil and pure turpentine as it would have made them too dark, so we coated them with heavy white sealer. Once we could see what colour this would bring it to we were able to decide on the stain required for the carcase. We stained the carcase with golden oak oil stain, and after drying the stained areas were coated with sealer.

We papered the carcase and drawers smooth with an old piece of grade 120 garnet paper. A few minor holes that looked bad we filled with a coloured beeswax.

We gave a few straight rubbers of thinned 4lb button polish to the whole job. We then put in the drawers to assess what colouring was required. From Fig. 88 (p. 78) you can see that there were a number of small areas that needed colouring – these were mainly where filler had been used.

We used a combination of colours but the basic ones were spirit red and black mixed into a 50:50 mix of button polish and methylated spirits. After colouring we applied a second coat of thin button polish to fix the colour. When this was dry we papered it down with an old piece of grade 150 garnet paper with some oil on it for lubrication.

The chest of drawers was finished relatively quickly with thin button polish, because we did not want there to be too great a build up of polish, but nonetheless wanted it to look fully polished. The finishing off sequence (the bodying up and finishing off stages became one and the same thing in this case because of the desire for a thin polish) was as follows:

1   one side and half the front
2   the other side and the other half of the front
3   the top
4   all the drawers together

We refitted the handles and gave the back of the carcase a coat of some old thin colour (usually dark) to make it look clean (Figs. 89, p. 79 and 126).

Fig 126   Front view of chest of drawers finished and fitted up

21

M ACCLESFIELD CHAIR

This chair dates from about 1760 and is called a Macclesfield chair because it was made in the town of Macclesfield, Cheshire, and has the distinguishing feature of an unusual top rail.

It is made of a combination of timbers as is common in country furniture. The timbers used include oak, ash and elm. The seat was not original. The reason for its state of collapse is that woodworm had got into several of the joints and eaten away much of the timber and glue around them. Woodworm will often attack old animal glue because it is sweet and generally easier to eat than the surrounding wood. Once they have eaten through the glue they will start on the timber. The woodwork attack on this chair was very recent (Fig. 127).

We had to replace two seat rails, one stretcher and the three ladders of the back because they were so badly attacked by worm. The seat could not be salvaged (Fig. 128).

Once repaired we treated the whole of the chair with a worm killer several times. We then washed down with ammonia water to clean it a little and to remove the greasy film left by the worm killer.

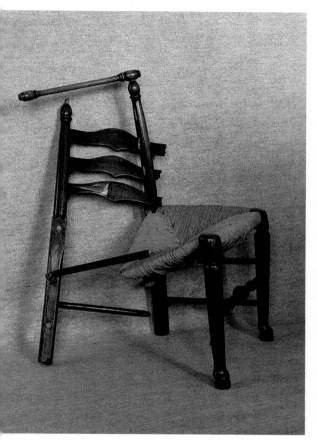

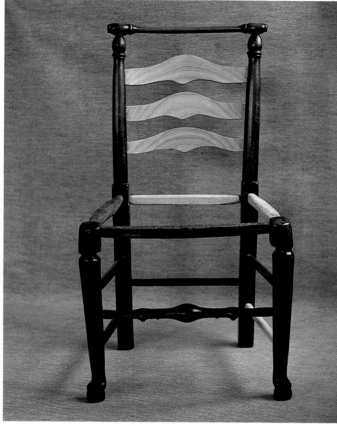

Fig 127 Macclesfield chair, the result of woodworm and a heavy dinner guest

Fig 128 Macclesfield chair fully repaired

We papered the chair all over with grade 120 garnet paper and then stained the new timber with a combination of dark oak and black oil stain. The chair was still dark after cleaning so a dark stain was needed.

After drying the stained pieces were sealed with heavy white sealer. After we papered the sealer we gave the whole chair a few rubbers of thinned 4lb button polish giving it a slight sheen so any necessary colouring could be seen.

The main areas requiring colouring were all the new pieces and a few small areas on the original wood. The main colours we used were spirit red and black and brown umber pigment.

After colouring we second-coated the new pieces only with thin button polish. When this was dry we papered it down with a sanding pad and gave a few rubbers to the whole chair making sure that the new pieces had as much polish on as the old. The chair was then re-rushed (Fig. 129).

Fig 129 Macclesfield chair ready for a delicate lady

22

AFRICAN WALNUT CHAIR

This well-made chair dates from the 1950s. It was mass produced and is made of African walnut in imitation Queen Anne style. The chair had probably been spray polished with cellulose lacquer which was fairly thick. The wood had faded and the customer wanted it made darker to match other furniture, and it also needed re-upholstering as some of the springs were hanging down under the chair (Fig. 130).

Our first job was to rip out the upholstery using a ripping chisel and a mallet. (For this job a dust mask should be worn because the dust from old upholstery is very fine and unpleasant). The chair was much easier to handle without the upholstery on (Figs. 131–132).

We stripped the wood using methyl chloride stripper, though it was sticky to get off as is common with old cellulose lacquer. We neutralized it with ammonia water to get as much of the old stain as possible out of the grain. It was now possible to see sappy edges in the timber that had been coloured out.

The chair was badly knocked about around the feet so we had to fill some holes, but there were only a few minor holes elsewhere. We first papered down

Fig 130   1950s walnut arm chair with original cover

Fig 131   1950s walnut arm chair minus cover

Fig 132   1950s walnut arm chair with the upholstery ripped out

with grade 80 garnet paper to remove a few deep scratches. The final grade of paper used was 120.

We stained the chair with a rosewood oil stain which made it a nice warm red colour that was not too dark. After the stain was dry we sealed with heavy white sealer. The sealer we papered smooth with a pad which was easier to use on the curves.

We then gave a few straight rubbers of thinned 4lb button polish so that it had a sheen and it was possible to see what colouring needed doing. There were a few sappy edges, mainly on the arms, and a few areas that had been filled with Brummer. The main colours we used were spirit red and black and brown umber.

We second coated the chair with a 50:50 mixture of pale amber varnish and 4lb button polish because a quick build and high shine was required. When dry (it is

Fig 133 1950s walnut arm chair, finished and reupholstered

so that all the grain was filled and there was a high shine. The chair was then reupholstered (Fig. 133).

best left to dry overnight as the varnish takes longer to dry than polish), we papered smooth with a pad.

We finished with special button polish

23

GEORGIAN MAHOGANY
CHEST OF DRAWERS

This chest of drawers, dating from c. 1780 and belonging to one of the authors, is mahogany with inlay and has unusual rosewood decoration on the drawers and top. It had had new back feet fitted in Victorian times and small pieces of the rosewood veneer were missing. It is all oak-lined and the drawer fronts were made in pine with brick construction.

We first stripped it down to the bare wood because at some stage it had been coated with varnish over dirt. It was repaired and papered with grade 120 garnet paper. We then stained with a 50:50 mixture of raw linseed oil and pure turpentine and left it to dry thoroughly.

We started the polishing stage with a brush coat of heavy white sealer; we papered down the sealer and the job was rubbered with thin button polish. Very little colouring was required as the timber was so well matched.

We then fixed the colour with a brush coat of thin button polish, which when hard we papered down with an old piece of oiled grade 150 garnet paper. Finishing off was quite straightforward using thin button polish until the result was a thin polish with the grain almost filled.

Fig 134 Detail of Georgian bow-fronted chest of drawers

We used thin French polish, i.e. 4lb button polish thinned down with an equal measure of methylated spirit. This was because we wanted the end result to be a thin finish as opposed to a full high shine. The result now, after four years of being waxed three times a year, is very pleasing and a joy to look at (Fig. 134).

24

M AHOGANY BUREAU

This attractive little Georgian mahogany bureau came to us to be repolished after it had been repaired by having new bracket feet fitted and several areas of cock beading renewed. However, the polish was in a very bad way as the bureau had been stored in a damp outhouse for sometime. It had to be stripped and repolished.

The bureau we took to pieces as follows:

1 all handles and escutcheons were removed
2 the lopers were taken out to make polishing easier
3 the fall was removed by unscrewing the hinges from the carcase, the hinges were left on the fall to make handling easier at the polishing stage
4 all the inside drawers, and the door, were taken out and their fittings were removed

The inside of the fall had the original skiver fitted which was in a poor condition but the customer wished to retain it. We therefore masked up the leather to avoid marking it with stripper. When masking up leather use low tack tape as the adhesive on ordinary masking tape is a little too strong and tends to pull the

Fig 135 Small Georgian mahogany bureau, open

1 inside compartment and the back of the fall

2 all the small drawers, the door and the lopers

3 all the main drawers

4 one side of the carcase

5 the other side of the carcase

6 the front of the carcase and the front of the fall

surface of the leather off.

We stripped the bureau in a logical manner, starting with the top first and then doing sections together:

In this manner we were not trying to tackle too large an area at a time and we could make sure it was all clean. The stripper was neutralized with ammonia water to remove old stain and dirt.

Several holes were filled with Brummer (plastic stopping). We then papered smooth starting with grade 80 garnet paper and finishing with grade 120.

Because of the natural beauty of the wood we decided to stain it with equal measures of raw linseed oil and pure turpentine. The new feet, however, we stained with an oil stain to get them to the same colour as the carcase. The stain we used was rosewood.

We left the stains to dry for 24 hours and then applied a coat of heavy white sealer. Because the fall had to be polished on both sides, we used bench pads in order to protect it (see Fig. 8, p. 22). When polishing double-sided items always polish the least important side first (in this case the inside) so that if you turn it over before it is fully dry only the less important side will be marked.

We papered down the sealer with a pad and gave three or four straight rubbers of button polish so that any necessary colouring could be carried out. The areas that needed colouring were where new pieces had been added, i.e. the feet and some areas of cock beading. They all needed darkening, and for this process we used spirit red, spirit black and some burnt sienna. We applied the colour with a number 6 Zorino mop.

We fixed the colour with a second coat of button polish. When hard, we papered the polish down with an old piece of oiled grade 150 garnet paper.

The bureau needed to be polished to a high shine with the grain filled so the bodying up and finishing off processes were carried out. It is necessary to divide the bureau into sections for polishing so that not too large an area is tackled at a time. Work in the following way by polishing:

1 the inside of the fall, all the small drawers, the door and the lopers
2 one side of the carcase and half the front
3 the other side and other half of the front
4 the inside compartment and the top
5 all the long drawers and the outside of the fall (allow the polish on the inside of the fall to harden for a few hours before turning it over)

We cleaned the handles by using an automotive chrome cleaner. The choice of metal cleaners is very large but we find that cream cleaners are better than the impregnated wadding cleaners available.

After allowing the polish to harden overnight we fitted the bureau up. The masking was removed from the fall and the leather was given a couple of rubbers of button polish to make it look fresher.

An interesting thing we found in this bureau was a secret drawer with two diaries from the 1940s, which the family did not know about – making them keener to have the piece back (Fig. 135).

25

REPRODUCTION OAK CABINET AND SIDEBOARD

These two reproduction oak pieces belong to the same customer; they had been quite dark and she wanted them lighter. Both pieces had been spray polished with coloured cellulose lacquer in such a way as to simulate age. Where the lacquer was scratched the bare wood showed through making both items look shabby.

We began by taking both items to pieces, which was quite a laborious task as there were many handles and hinges, particularly on the sideboard. The system of stripping was much the same as with other pieces:

1 top
2 one side
3 the other side
4 the front and the drawers
5 the doors

We had to apply the stripper liberally as the cellulose soaked it up very quickly. More coats of stripper had to be applied until the whole area being stripped stayed wet.

We scraped the lacquer off quite easily when soft but it was very sticky. In the carved areas it was not possible to use a scraper so we used a wire brush and steel wool. Once stripped we neutralized both

Fig 137 Reproduction oak sideboard

items with ammonia water in order to get rid of the traces of stripper in all the nooks and crannies.

The oak papered down easily, starting with grade 80 garnet paper and finishing with grade 120. We stained both the sideboard and the cabinet with golden oak oil stain and left them to dry for several hours. We were not required to make them look old by distressing them as the customer wanted them to look light in colour and like new pieces again.

We sealed the stain with heavy white sealer, and used a pad to smooth the dry sealer because it made it easier to get into the carvings.

We then gave three or four rubbers to both jobs and they were then ready for colouring. They were loosely assembled so we could assess what colouring was required.

Fig 136 Reproduction oak cabinet

As both pieces were to be in the same room, it was important that we coloured them to match each other as well as colouring out any light marks or rails.

The main colours we used were spirit red, spirit black and brown umber. Several areas needed colouring on both pieces, i.e. horizontal rails on many of the doors. We coated the colour with a number 6 Zorino mop and when all colouring was completed the pieces were ready for second coating. The bases, doors and drawers of both pieces we second coated with button polish and both tops were coated with heat resisting pale polish.

When the polishes were hard we papered them down with a pad. The bases, doors and drawers were finished off with a few stiff rubbers of button polish. Because the tops had been coated with heat resisting pale polish we had to finish with it. Again a few stiff rubbers were all that was required. Upon re-assembly both pieces of furniture looked better than new (Figs. 136–137).

26

MAHOGANY TRIPOD TABLE

This little mahogany tripod table was bought in Washington state and cost £17 ($30) in an antique shop. As all the materials were to hand it was easy for us to strip and repolish it. It had been polished with a modern cellulose type lacquer which was in poor condition and the only remedy was to remove it and start again.

We stripped the top first which allowed the bottom to be held if required. The bottom was then stripped as soon as the top was dry enough to hold. The table stripped quite easily and we neutralized it with turpentine substitute as there was no ammonia to hand.

We papered it down with grade 80 and then grade 100 garnet paper. Because a natural colour was required we stained it with an equal measure mixture of raw linseed oil and pure turpentine.

After leaving to dry for twenty four hours we sealed the table with a coat of heavy white sealer. When dry the sealer was papered with a pad. We then applied three or four rubbers of button polish before assessing the colouring.

No colouring was required as the timber was surprisingly well matched. We second coated the base with 4lb button polish

Fig 138 Mahogany tripod table

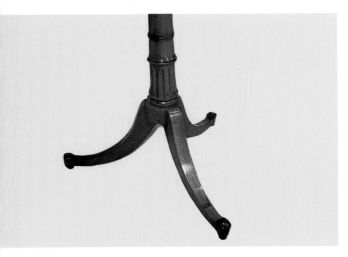

then coated the top with heat resisting pale polish.

When the polishes were hard we papered smooth with a pad. The bottom was finished first with button polish, then the grain was choked and polished to a high shine. We finished the top with heat resisting pale polish to the same degree of shine as the base (Figs. 138–139).

Fig 139   Mahogany tripod table, detail

27

STAIRCASE

If you wish to polish a new staircase it is always easier to stain and polish it whilst in pieces as it is more manageable. Therefore, if you wish to strip and repolish an existing fitted staircase dismantle it if possible. Whatever you do, never try to polish a staircase when the surrounding walls have been newly decorated. The time to stain and polish a staircase *in situ* is when the hall has been stripped prior to redecorating.

This staircase was part original and part new. The newels, handrails and panelling were original and all the balusters were new as the previous owners of the house had fitted wrought iron work in place of the original balusters. The acorn cappings for the newels, the sole plate (or stringing capping) and the baluster spacers were also new. The handrails and newels were the original polished oak and the pine panelling had been painted cream.

Stripping

The whole house was being refurbished when we were called in so there was no carpet or wallpaper to worry about. We placed dust sheets on the floors and stairs to make sure we kept the resulting dirt in

a confined area. We started by stripping at the top of the staircase, i.e. half newel, newels and handrails, working from top to bottom since if any stripper splashed below it would fall onto work requiring stripping. If we had started from the bottom and worked upwards we might have splashed areas we had already finished stripping and which we wanted to keep as clean as possible. We worked with all the doors and windows open to ensure good ventilation.

The vertical panelling was very difficult to strip as it had 80 years of paint and scumble on it. We applied stripper as liberally as possible, considering how easily it ran off, and we rewetted the work several times until the paint started to bubble. We scraped off the paint with a paint scraper and put the waste into newspaper. More stripper was applied and we again removed the paint with a paint scraper. Yet more stripper was applied but this time we were able to remove the softened paint with grade 3 steel wool. By this stage the surface was quite clean of the old paint.

We neutralized the whole staircase with a small amount of 0.880 ammonia in hot water. It was applied liberally to a small area at a time and we rubbed it vigorously with a clean piece of grade 3 steel wool in the direction of the grain.

Preparation and staining

We papered smooth all the staircase, old and new, in preparation for staining. The panelling required a lot of papering in order to get it even and to remove small amounts of paint lodged in corners and

Fig 140   A staircase – the newels, handrail and panelling are original and the balusters and acorns are new

moulds. We filled several small holes with a plastic stopping.

The original oak was stained first to give us the basic colour to work to. We stained it with golden oak which gave a warm light oak colour. The new pieces of oak, i.e. the acorns, we also stained with the same stain. The hemlock balusters and the pine panelling were stained with a combination of golden oak and dark oak in order to darken them a little to match the original oak. We added only a small amount of dark oak otherwise the warmth would have been 'killed'.

The balusters and acorns were still to be fitted at this stage which made the staining easier. After the stain had dried we gave all the pieces a coat of heavy white sealer. When this was dry we smoothed it down with a pad and then gave four rubbers of 4lb button polish to all pieces. Several of the balusters were put temporarily into place in order to assess for colouring.

Polishing

Several small areas on the handrail and some larger areas on the panelling required colouring where holes had been filled. In order to colour, we made a 50:50 mix of methylated spirit and button polish and small amounts of spirit red, spirit black and raw sienna were added. We applied the colour with a swan's quill to the required areas.

We second coated all the pieces with 4lb button polish in order to fix the colour and to give a good body of polish on which to finish. When the polish was hard we papered it smooth with a pad. Several stiff rubbers were given to all pieces as a very high shine was not required.

The staircase was assembled by the joiners the following day when everything

was ready to handle. We would normally expect to return to a staircase to fill any holes and do any touching up. Very often the spacer pieces will be glued and pinned into position so the holes need filling with coloured beeswax and then rubbering over.

Whilst in the customers' house doing the staircase we were asked to do an oak fire surround and the oak french windows and window seat in a lounge (Figs. 140–141).

Fig 141   A staircase – the new hemlock balusters
match well with the original oak

28

*F*IRE SURROUND

When stripping and repolishing a fire surround we would normally remove it and take it into pieces as it makes the job easier and produces a better finish. In this case we were not able to remove it as it was well plastered into the wall. Fortunately all the wallpaper had been removed so we did not need to worry about marking the surrounding area.

We started stripping the surround from the top downwards. There was not much polish on it so once we had applied the stripper we were able to remove the softened polish with grade 3 steel wool. We did not need to use a paint scraper as there was so little material on it.

After stripping we neutralized it with a small amount of 0.880 ammonia in hot water. The ammonia water was applied liberally to small areas and then rubbed with grade 3 steel wool to remove all final traces of dirt and stripper.

When the ammonia water had dried we filled several holes with a plastic stopper. Once the stopper was dry we

Fig 142 An oak fireplace, which had to be stripped and repolished *in situ*. It was stained with a golden oak stain which gave a pleasant warm colour

papered the surround smooth with garnet paper – we started with grade 80 and finished with grade 120.

Our customer required the fire surround to be the same colour as the staircase so we stained it with golden oak oil stain. When this was dry we sealed it with a brush coat of heavy white sealer. We smoothed the sealer with a sanding pad as it was easier to use than garnet paper in the moulds and other awkward areas.

We then gave about four rubbers of thinned 4lb button polish to the surround and assessed the colouring. Only small areas required colouring, mainly where filler had been used. The colours we used were the same as for the staircase – spirit red, spirit black and raw sienna.

The surround was second coated with heat resisting pale polish. We used this polish because of the proximity to heat when the fire is in use. When the polish was hard we smoothed it with a pad and gave a few stiff rubbers of thinned heat resisting pale polish in order to achieve the required result (Fig. 142).

29

*F*RENCH WINDOW AND WINDOW SEATS

Before starting to strip any of the wood we removed the doors and took off all the door furniture. We had to put the doors back on each evening, so we had to plan our work in order that the doors would be at a suitable stage for rehanging at the end of each day, i.e. they could not be wet with stain or polish. The doors had to be stripped on both sides as the outsides were to be varnished with yacht varnish to protect them from the elements.

We covered up the glass in the doors on both sides to avoid marking them with stain or polish. For this we used masking tape and newspaper. At the same time we also put masking tape around the windows in the windowseat area and around the floor to avoid marking the parquet floor. There were also several light switches and plug sockets that we had to mask up with tape.

We placed dust sheets on the floor to protect it and to collect all the dust etc. in them. Because we were working in the summer we were able to place the doors on trestles outside and work on them there. Also, as the doors were off we had plenty of ventilation.

We stripped the doors first (bearing in mind the need to rehang them) and then started on the window seats and the surrounding areas. We applied stripper as liberally as possible bearing in mind that there were a lot of vertical areas. As with the fire surround there was not much polish on the oak so it was not necessary to use a paint scraper but only grade 3 steel wool.

After all stripping had been done we neutralized all areas with a small amount of 0.880 ammonia in hot water. Small areas were neutralized at a time and then rubbed clean with a fresh piece of grade 3 steel wool. When the ammonia water had dried we filled numerous small holes with plastic stopper.

We papered the doors smooth first and then the other areas. We stained the oak with a golden oak oil stain in order to match to the fire surround. This constituted the end of one days work for the two of us and we were then able to rehang the doors.

As the stain had been able to dry overnight we were able to carry on the next day with sealing. The first task on arriving at the house was to remove the doors and coat one side of each of the doors with heavy white sealer. Whilst that was drying we coated the remaining areas. When we had finished sealing everything we were able to turn the doors over and coat the other sides.

We smoothed the dry sealer with a pad as it was easier to use on shaped and moulded areas than garnet paper. A few straight rubbers of thinned 4lb button polish were given to all areas. We first rubbered one side of each of the doors, then the rest of the job and lastly the other side of the doors.

After all areas had been rubbered we placed the doors in position in order to check for colouring. The cross rails to the outside of the doors were lighter so

required colouring. Other areas needing colouring were where filler had been used and where the timber had been exposed to a lot of light. A reasonable amount of 50:50 methylated spirit and button polish was mixed and to this the necessary colours were added. Colours required were spirit red, spirit black and a small amount of brown umber. We ensured we mixed a reasonable amount of colour as we had a substantial amount to colour. We used a swan's quill to colour the areas where filler had been used. For the larger areas we used a number 6 Zorino mop.

After all areas had been coloured we fixed it with a brush coat of 4lb button polish, i.e. second coat. We coated one side of each door first (having replaced them on the trestles first), then the seats etc. and lastly the other side of each door. This constituted the end of the second day's work for two. We again had to rehang the doors.

The next day we started by taking the doors off and placing them on trestles. All areas were smoothed with a pad in preparation for finishing off. A high build of polish was not required so all that was needed was a few straight rubbers of thinned 4lb button polish. The outside of the doors required finishing with yacht varnish. We finished the inside of the doors first, then the remaining areas. The outsides of the doors we coated with yacht varnish, and as this is slow drying, we had to wait for quite a while before we were able to handle them for rehanging.

Whilst we were waiting for the varnish to dry we removed all masking tape and made sure that the glass and the floor were clean. We rehung the doors before they were fully dry but the customer was able to keep the door open long enough for them to dry. That ended the third day.

Fig 143 A lounge with French windows and window seats in oak. The doors were removed in order to work on them but all other pieces remained fixed which made stripping difficult

The following day one of us returned to paper down the outside of the door and varnish it again. There was no need to remove the doors this time as the greater part of the work had already been done (Fig. 143).

30

*P*INE DOORS

If any door is to be stripped and repolished
it is easier (and in many ways essential)
that the door is taken off its hinges first.
This allows you to lie the door down and
thus make the job of working on it all the
more easy. If you are removing several
doors to work on at once be sure to mark
which door comes from where. Always
mark the top edge of the door with chisel
marks and the hinge edge of the door case.

Once the door is loose remove all door
furniture, e.g. handles, finger plates, locks
if fitted to the outside of the door and
hinges. Lie the door down on trestles of
appropriate height and apply stripper
liberally. If stripping off paint there will
probably be many years accumulation so
it will take a lot of stripper and hard work
to remove it.

The doors in this chapter are 1930s
pitch pine internal doors which had been
modernized in the 1960s by the addition
of hardboard and timber moulds to make
them look plainer; they also had unattrac-
tive handles which needed replacing.
The moulds and hardboard were easily
removed by placing a broad chisel under
the hardboard and gently prising the board
away from the door. Some nails remained

in the door after the hardboard was removed and we extracted these with pliers.

We laid the doors on trestles and applied stripper. Because the weather was fine at the time, we were able to do all the stripping and timber preparation outside. If you wish to tackle doors always work in a well-ventilated area or better still outside. We coated the stripper generously as there was much paint to remove. The stripper soon dried up so we applied more until all the paint had softened and bubbled. We used a paint scraper to remove the softened paint which was placed in newspaper; this resulted in the removal of the worst of the paint. Stripper was applied liberally again and was removed with grade 3 steel wool in order to get the paint out of all the corners and moulds. When both sides of the doors had been stripped we neutralized them with ammonia water and rubbed them clean with a piece of grade 3 steel wool.

It is possible to have doors dipped in hot caustic soda in order to remove the paint but care should be taken if doing this as dipping can cause problems. Never dip timbers such as walnut, mahogany or oak as it can dramatically darken the colour of the timber. Pine is the best timber to dip and was frequently the most painted one. Never dip an item whose joints are loose as the process will generally weaken the glue if it is starting to perish and **never** dip veneered items as there is a great likelihood that the veneer will be removed as the glue holding it in place is softened.

Almost any suitable painted item can be dipped provided it can be fitted into a caustic tank, but always choose a reputable firm of dippers as some may leave items in for too long and so cause unnecessary problems. It is not normally necessary to have polished items dipped

Fig 144   The sequence for sanding, staining and polishing a door is illustrated in this diagram and should always be adhered to in order to achieve the best results. The sequence for stripping is not as vital but it would be best to do the moulds and panels first and then the rest of the door

as there is not the same build up of material with polish as there is with paint.

Once the ammonia water had dried out, we filled any holes with either plastic stopper or epoxy filler and carried out any repairs. We then papered the doors smooth, starting with grade 80 garnet paper and finishing with grade 120. The best sequence to follow is to paper the panels and moulds then the cross rails and finally the uprights. If this sequence is adopted for staining, rubbing and coating then problems will be minimized (Fig. 144).

PINE DOORS

149

The doors needed to be as light as possible, so staining was not required. After papering, we sealed the doors with heavy white sealer which brought them up to a pleasant nut brown colour. We smoothed the sealer with a pad as this was easier than using garnet paper in the moulds. We gave about four straight rubbers of thinned 4lb button polish all over, following the sequence of panels and moulds, then crossrails and finally up-rights. Leave a reasonable amount of time before turning the door over to ensure that the polish has hardened sufficiently. Once the door has received four rubbers stand it up and check whether any colouring is required. On these doors there were innumerable pin holes that had been filled and needed colouring. We used a 50:50 mixture of button polish and methylated spirit with colours added. The colours required were spirit red and spirit black and occasionally a little brown umber where marks were particularly light.

After colouring the doors, we second coated them with a brush coat of 4lb button polish. When this was dry it was papered smooth with a pad and a few straight rubbers of thinned 4lb button polish were given in order to produce a satisfactory finish. As the doors are pine a great build up was not required so with about four straight rubbers we finished the job.

Fig 145 A 1930s pitch pine door, repolished

CONCLUSION

When writing this book we felt that we had encountered a challenge, which was to encourage and help anyone interested in woodwork or furniture to obtain very satisfying polishing results, and to be able to solve problems as they arise. We hope we have succeeded in this and trust the book will give many potential polishers all the information they need to start learning to French polish, and will prove a valuable practical reference guide for all those who are polishing already. We have written this book so you can pick out points of interest from the desired chapters, but in conclusion, we would particularly like to stress the following.

French polishing should be an enjoyable and relaxing job, so if you become frustrated by any difficulties put the piece you are working on to one side and do something totally different; then you can come back to the job later, with fresh eyes and a keener interest.

One thing in particular which will require a good deal of thought and practice is the making of a rubber. The line drawings in Chapter 12 are the best you will see on the subject, so go through them slowly and frequently until you can make and keep the desired shape, because this is the key to successful polishing, and once you have perfected this art it will make the rest of French polishing seem easy.

We hope we have encouraged you sufficiently to take up or improve your French polishing. The results you can achieve for yourself can be most rewarding – but don't forget that to make a really good polisher you need patience, and lots of practice!

Further information

Courses

To help perfect your techniques and talk over any problems, courses offering hands-on tuition can be extremely helpful. We run courses jointly at our workshops in Cheshire, and individually elsewhere. For more information, please telephone or write to:

Alan Waterhouse and Philippa Barstow
Unit H3
Newton Business Park
Talbot Road
Hyde
Cheshire SK14 4UQ
(Tel: 061 3684075)

John Boddy's Fine Wood and Tool Store
Riverside Sawmills
Boroughbridge
N Yorks YO5 9LJ
(Tel: 0423 332370)

Craft Supplies
The Mill
Millers Dale
Nr Buxton
Derbyshire SK17 8SN
(Tel: 0298 871832)

Shows

Local and national woodworking shows are good places to see demonstrations of woodfinishing and to pick up tips and ask questions. We always have a stand at The International Practical Woodworking Show, held each spring at the Wembley Exhibition Centre, and are always very glad to answer any questions and give advice. For details see *Practical Woodworking* magazine.

Further Reading

The woodwork magazines, in particular *Practical Woodworking*, *Woodworker* and *Traditional Woodworking*, often have interesting articles on different aspects of woodfinishing and furniture. In addition, we recommend the following books:

John Bly, *Discovering English Furniture*, Shire Publications, 1976
Herbert Cescinsky, *English Furniture from Gothic to Sheraton*, Dover Publications, 1986
Charles Hayward, *English Period Furniture*, Bell & Hyman, 1984
Charles Hayward, *Staining and Polishing*, Bell & Hyman, 1983

French Polishing – *the video*

We have produced a video to complement this book, which covers all the French polishing techniques and the problems you might encounter. Published by Find A Fact Limited, and available from Alan Waterhouse and Philippa Barstow, address as above, or alternatively from:

Find A Fact Ltd
15 Green Close
Uley
near Dursley
Gloucestershire

U.S.A. MATERIALS

Paint stripper

Bulldog Brand
Dullfix
TM-4
Zipp-Off

Woodworm destruction

Pentide
Wood Life
Xylamon
Decay-not

Furniture polish

Johnson's
Kahn's prepared wax

Furniture creams & liquid polishes

Johnson's
Minwax

S UPPLIERS

BRITISH AND IRISH

Alan Waterhouse and Philippa Barstow
Unit H3
Newton Business Park
Talbot Road
Hyde
Cheshire
SK14 4UQ
England
Tel: 0161 3684075   *Fax:* 0161 3684075

**Polish manufacturer (also supply
stains, wadding, brushes etc)**

F T Morrell and Co. Ltd
Mill Lane
Woodley, Stockport
Cheshire
SK6 1RN
England

Tel: 0161 4302292   *Fax:* 0161 4066276

F T Morrell & Co. Ltd
Morrell Court
Brownfields
Welwyn Garden City
Hertfordshire
AL7 1AY
England

Tel: 01707 362400   *Fax:* 01707 293541

F T Morrell and Co. Ltd,
John F Kennedy Drive
Bluebell
Dublin 12
Eire

Tel: 01 505095/505187   *Fax:* 01 504188

Distributors for F K Morrell and Co. Ltd

UK Distributors

Richard Berry
Unit 1
Chapel Place
North Street
Portslade
Brighton
England

Tel: 01273 419471   *Fax:* 01273 421925

M.B.K. Surface Coatings Ltd
Taylor Lane
Loscoe
Derbyshire
England

Tel: 01773 769771   *Fax:* 01773 530078

M.B.K. Surface Coatings Ltd
Unit 5
Coulson Street Industrial Estate
Spennymoor
County Durham
England

Tel: 01388 812658   *Fax:* 01388 816201

McMillan Brothers
19B Fairley Street
Ibrox
Glasgow
G51 2SN
Scotland

Tel: 0141 4274298   *Fax:* 0141 4273996

Ireland Distributors

Jetspray Ltd
Currabunny
Carrigaline
County Cork
Eire

Tel: 010 353 21378198
Fax: 010 353 121378049

D F Ross and Sons Ltd
34 Maghberry Road
Maghberry Moira
County Armagh
Northern Ireland

Tel: 01846 611461   *Fax:* 01846 611891

Manufacturers of Briwax (and suppliers of polishing materials)

Henry Flack Ltd
Borough Works
Elmers End
Beckenham
England

Tel: 0181 6582299

Manufacturers of abrasive pads

Sandmaster Ltd
Airfield Industrial Estate
Hixon
Stafford
ST18 0PF
England

Tel: 01889 270695   *Fax:* 01889 271161

Suppliers of abrasive papers

Anglo Abrasives Ltd
Unit 1
Barlow Street
Walkden
Manchester
M28 5BN
England

Tel: 0161 7908241

Suppliers of tooled leathers and skivers

Rosemary Evans
Antique Leathers
4 Berwyn Close
Marchwiel
Wrexham
Clwyd
LL13 0PT
Wales

Tel: 01978 354400

U.S.A.

Manufacturers of Briwax (and suppliers of finishing materials)

Henry Flack International Inc.
18333 Preston Road
Suite 460
Dallas
Texas 75252
USA

Tel: 214 407 9172   *Fax:* 214 407 9622
    800 527 4929

Finishing materials

Garret Wade Co.
161 Avenue of the Americas
New York
New York 10013

Mohawk Finishing Products Inc.
Amsterdam
New York
New York 12010

Leather

Roberts Leather Studios Inc.
214 West 29th Street
Unit 403
New York
New York 10001

Berman Leathercraft Inc.
145 South Street
Boston
Massachusetts 0211

*I*NDEX